LOVE OF HAVING:
Compulsive Buying, Spending, and Hoarding

By

George R. Ingham, Ph.D., L.I.C.S.W.

Contents

Preface

It is no measure of health to be well adjusted to a sick society.
—Krishnamurti

How many people ruin themselves by laying out
money on trinkets of frivolous utility? ... All
their pockets are stuffed with little conveniences.
They continue new pockets unknown in the
clothes of other people, in order to carry a
greater number.
—Adam Smith, *Theory of Moral Sentiments*

Alcoholism, compulsive gambling, heroin dependence, there are some behaviors that a person who does not suffer from them has a hard time fully understanding. But, there is another group of behaviors, compulsive buying, spending, and hoarding that those of us who live in capitalist countries can easily relate to. Who among us has never gone shopping just to lift our spirits. Most of us understand the phrase Retail Therapy, and the common refrain: when the going gets tough, the tough go shopping. Yet studies show that most people make impulse purchases when they are in a positive mood, one reason for the soothing music in most stores and malls. What does this tell us about the causes of compulsion and addiction, and who is at greatest risk of developing a dependency? How many of us have felt bad about a purchase, or have hidden it from our spouse rather than face his or her reproach. And yet, guilt can be a motivating strategy for many to help them avoid excessive spending. Getting rid of an object becomes impossible when we tell ourselves that we just might have some use for it in some distant future. If, perchance, we are forced to move, we soon become aware of the vast hoard of stuff we have managed to accumulate in our lives, much of it of no apparent use. Who has not had the experience of having someone close to them, a parent or a spouse perhaps, throw away something highly valued, that was seen by them as only being trash. How many of us live in constant fear of losing their home or having their electricity cutoff because of overspending and household budgets that are out of control.

We are all conscious, on some level, that the objects we purchase have taken on psychological value, and that they exert some control over the course of our life. William James (1890) was one of the first psychologists to note that modern men and women tend to define themselves, at least in part, by the possessions they own. We also have a growing awareness that our

4

present level of consumption is unsustainable for the world and our own homes. The code words, clutter bug, may not apply; we may not believe that our shopping or hoarding behavior is addictive; but, in our most reflective moments, we are aware that such behavior is detrimental to our overall well-being.

On Black Friday, the day after Thanksgiving, large groups of perfectly normal people behave as if they have been possessed by a shopping demon. Such a frenzy of grasping and shoving has led, not infrequently, to injury, even death. What's more, most people can identify with some of the motives behind such behavior. We live in a society where a statement such as, what kind of commodity are you, is actually considered reasonable. A society where our leaders are evaluated, not for their values or character, but for what is called their brand, as well as by the type and quantity of objects they own. Most of us have no problem relating when one woman, with an admitted shopping problem, explains that she just wanted to experience herself as "better than" she was; and, therefore, she bought luxury goods. She would imagine that the sales people would think of her as rich and famous.[1]

The fact that most people in our culture can empathize, to some extent, with this behavior, points to a common element in our socialization. The extent to which problems related to control of our desires or impulses lead to different types of behavior depending on a person's gender or culture has been widely noted. To what extent is it true that women are shoppers, men are buyers, or is this just one more example of men labeling women in order to control them. Our popular culture has even produced television channels devoted to watching hoarders, A&E's *Hoarders* and TLC's *Hoarding: Buried Alive*, something reminiscent of the public display of mentally ill patients for entertainment in early modern Europe[2] Ironically, the very need to be sensational, manipulative, and melodramatic, utilized by reality TV, is driven by the same consumer value system behind our acquisitive society. It can, and sometimes does, lead to psychic harm. The one redeeming positive benefit that has come from these programs has been an increased awareness and understanding of a problem that had been largely hidden and misunderstood.

The use of the label, hoarder, is, itself, deeply problematic, as it reifies a behavior. One peer support group uses the title Finders and Keepers. On the other hand, just as Laura's collection of glass objects, in *The Glass Menagerie,* "takes up a good deal of [her] time," and symbolizes deep psychic pain, so the kind of collecting involved in these behaviors can destroy fortunes, relations, and even lives. If, as I will argue, we all fit somewhere on a continuum from "normal" to "pathological" consumer behavior, what are the exact criteria that determine where we cross a line, assuming that there is such a line, into behaviors that can be labeled "compulsive" or even "addictive".

Despite strong evidence of an onset before the age of twenty, little attention has been paid to early intervention and prevention of hoarding problems, including social and cultural influences. However, the fact that hoarding disorder has been identified in all cultures and at all times clearly points to a need to look beyond our consumer culture if we are to fully understand

and treat this problem. Although compulsive acquisition of objects is often a major feature, difficulties with discarding or departing with these objects is a defining characteristic of hoarding disorder. In addition to cognitive, neurological, and, possibly, genetic factors, issues relating to attachment and early loss clearly play an important causative role in the development of problems with hoarding. Attachment is not only, as Simone Weil noted, "the great fabricator of illusions," it is also the greatest source of pain when it involves the loss of personal relations. The withdrawal and social isolation seen with those suffering from hoarding disorder is, therefore, both a causal factor and also an effect of their hoarding, especially since it can bring with it the shame that often results from hoarding behavior.

It was not that long ago that consumer behavior labeled abnormal was thought to be rare, and mostly confined to the rich and famous, like Jacqueline Kennedy Onassis and Imelda Marcos. Since I first wrote about this topic in the nineteen eighties, a flood of studies, books, and articles have appeared. They represent, in part, an awareness that our culture has contributed to an epidemic of unhealthy shopping behavior. In light of social research, it has become nearly impossible to accept the economic shibboleth that the only role of advertising is to provide the consumer with the information necessary for making a good choice; just helping her to get what she already wants.

At the same time, there has been a significant shift in the field of psychiatry, away from a restrictively medical view of illness to a growing awareness of the importance of context, and a more holistic approach to healthy living and psychological hygiene. Critics have argued against the very idea of medicalizing such consumer behaviors as compulsive buying and hoarding.[3] It is no longer considered radical to question whether or not the role of therapy should be to help sufferers learn to adapt to and internalize cultural norms that may be damaging to their overall well-being. The recent controversy over the inclusion of hoarding in the latest edition of the *Diagnostic and Statistical Manual* is deliciously ironic in that at least part of the motivation for such medicalization of extreme consumer behaviors comes from the desire to sell something, namely psychotherapy services and psychoactive medications. The huge increase in studies of such behaviors has come, largely, from psychologists who work for consumer research firms. There is even a discipline called neuromarketing, which utilizes the new neuroimaging techniques to try and influence the buying experience. Also, these diagnostic criteria, even my own suggestions, are purely operational and experiential, rather than causal, in nature. At the same time, there has also been a growing recognition that such complex human behaviors as compulsive buying, spending, and hoarding, can only be fully understood using an interdisciplinary approach.

The issues involved in these recent studies and writings are profound: how do we define well-being and a healthy lifestyle; what is the true definition of personal autonomy and how does it differ from addiction; how do we distinguish between our desires and our needs; what should be the role of culture and government in promoting healthy economic behavior; and how should we define illness. It is important to distinguish between two separate capacities of a healthy will: the ability to recognize our natural needs, and the capacity to choose between our needs and desires[4]

This book borrows the very useful definitions of need and want offered by Christian Bay (1968), but with important modifications, in order to delineate the role of society and culture in promoting or helping to prevent consumer disorders.

It is truly remarkable the degree to which scientific research in this area seems to confirm ancient wisdom about how to live a healthy and productive life. The recent increased focus on human flourishing and a sense of personal well-being has led to a critical assessment of cultural impediments to good mental health.[5] There is a growing awareness that the role of government should not be to inflame desire and encourage the spread of addictive behaviors, but to build social institutions that help foster self-control and develop the capacity to defer gratification. It may be that we can disagree as to whether or not the state should be allowed to force its citizens to be free and autonomous, for example through compulsive education, but we should all agree that fostering dependency or addiction in its citizens should not be the role of a free society. In his highly relevant essay, "Man the Reformer," Emerson showed how, in a free society, what we

choose to consume can make us complicit in harm to others. Pope
Francis has called attention to how this situation has only gotten
worse with a global economy.[6] The same moral dilemma also
applies, not only to what, but also to how much we consume.

The use of the term, 'materialism' has become popular with
marketing experts and others, to summarize findings from a
number of scientific studies that show a strong negative relation
between certain values and all aspects of good mental health,
freedom, and real human flourishing.[7] These studies have
contributed greatly to a fuller understanding of the relationship
between our ideas and values and a strong and fulfilling life. For
example, they have shown that it is positive experiences that
people tend to remember, rather than the objects they happened to
have purchased. However, the term materialism itself carries
certain problematic religious and other historical connotations, and
it fails to capture the active dispositional aspect of pathological
consumer behavior.

This book argues that compulsive shopping,
spending, and hoarding are extreme examples of a general

disposition, with the Greek word *pleonexia* (excessive

acquisitiveness) used as a more accurate and convenient

descriptive term than such words as shopaholic or compulsive

hoarder .[8] This disposition was recognized as detrimental for

healthy well-being in most cultures and at most times in history.[9] It

has only been nurtured or encouraged in certain western cultures

since the eighteenth century. Pleonexia is seen as a complex,

habitual, impulsive behavior which attempts to maintain order and

continuity in the sense of self. It represents a failure in self-

cohesion, an attempt to counter feelings of emptiness created by

the fragmentation and objectification of desire in our commodity

culture. Such internal functions as regulation of feelings, self-

esteem, as well as non-harmful techniques of self-soothing are

what become pathological in pleonexia. Diagnosis, as well as denial,

tend to revolve around the question of what is "excessive", "when is

enough, enough?"[10] However, it is the insatiability of unregulated

desire that has long been recognized as the most destructive element

in these behaviors, as well as the anxiety engendered by the need "to

acquire and keep possessions that one might lose or fail to obtain."[11]

For an individual with this disorder, the concepts of adequate, sufficient or abundant are foreign. There is always the need for more.[12]

There are significant differences, which it is important to distinguish, between compulsive acquiring, spending, and hoarding. Shortly after I began writing about hoarding I turned on the local news to a report of a fatal house fire, in which the firemen were hampered from rescuing the elderly occupants because of extreme clutter. Most local fire captains would agree with the one quoted in this case, when he asserted that "hoarding is one of the most dangerous things we deal with. When you're looking for somebody, when you can't tell what's the walls and what's the stairwell, it's so dangerous. And it's more prevalent than you think."[13] Even though death may not be the usual outcome of this disorder, personal, child, and communal safety is a very common concern, and there are enough examples of sufferers being literally buried alive to warrant society's attention. Of course, many individuals suffer from a combination of these disorders, as well as from other mental health problems, such as anxiety and depression. It is, therefore, very important to understand why certain individuals are at greater risk for developing these disorders of behavior. Given the central causative role of values and beliefs, a cognitive-behavioral approach to therapy can be most efficacious. However, it will be seen that a psychodynamic approach, properly understood, can also help to explain and treat these behavioral problems. The treatment methods recommended here draw on an updated version of the relational approach of Erich Fromm and certain members of the William Alanson White Institute. They have the virtue of being contextualist, taking into consideration the psychological effects of the neoliberal economic values that have crept into every area of our society, including, alas, the therapeutic community.[14] Neurological deficits, especially problems with information processing, may also play an important role in making a person vulnerable to these disorders, especially with hoarding.[15] There is strong evidence indicating that hoarding disorder results from a pathological exaggeration of innate tendencies we all carry. For this and other reasons, it has also been found that behavioral and cognitive/behavioral treatment methods can be among the most effective in helping those relatively few individuals who recognize that they have a problem and seek help. But, ours is a culture in which many parents choose to give their children possessions as their only sign of affection. It should not be surprising, therefore, that denial, in all its complex forms, plays a major role in preventing sufferers from recognizing the true cause of their problem.

The question of personal freedom of action is central to the analysis. The realization that control of one's appetites and desires is essential for good mental health goes back at least to the ancient Greeks. The causal importance of false beliefs and judgments has also been known since antiquity.[16] However, it has only been with the advent of modern psychiatry and neurology that these earlier insights have lost their moralistic overtones. The amount of psychic energy and precious time spent on compulsive behavior contributes to the definition of one form of dependency, which has been labeled "existential."[17] The substitution of manipulation for self-control is a central feature of the addictive pattern in the individual and the family structure. In his important little book on power, the social and political scientist, Steven Lukes, broadens our understanding of additional methods of "influencing, shaping or determining [our] very wants," beyond simple manipulation.[18] The goal of psychotherapy, that is argued for here, is similar to the concept of "positive freedom" described by Charles Taylor, one in which an individual fails to be fully free to the extent that she lacks self-control and self-realization (1986). Bernard Berofsky's (1995) sophisticated analysis of personal autonomy is applied to the psychological issues important here. This form of analysis has the virtue of demonstrating the connection between the social and cultural influences on the individual's psychic impairment, while recognizing the possible dangers involved when so-called experts distinguish between needs and wants.[19]

The importance of this aspect of the problem has been increasing as more areas of our life have come under the influence of an acquisitive value system, and as our culture and government engage in more and more actions that promote such dependence. This process has been bolstered by an industry of psychological experts, armed with the latest research findings on how to create illusory and magical cures for the empty self that they helped to

17

foster. If democracy is to survive this age of technology, citizens will need to be educated, from an early age, on how to detect and resist propaganda. The responsibility of a good government, in this important area, is supported by no less an authority of capitalism than Adam Smith. My use of the term **self** follows the definition given by Stephen Greenblatt: "a sense of personal order, a characteristic mode of address to the world, a structure of bounded desires."[20] This definition harkens to an old and venerable ideal conception of a well-ordered personality and commonwealth. Chapter 2, is concerned with this question of possible *external* coercion; that is, manufactured desire, or what is labeled with the strongly evaluative title, the *manipulationist* thesis. If one takes this thesis too literally, then to pathologize consumer behavior would be a clear example of what Philip Cushman calls "blaming the victim."[21]. This thesis, however, fails to take into consideration the degree to which coercion, like freedom, is a complex concept, with different degrees of subtlety and power to influence behavior. We can all agree that a person who lacks the capacity to avoid certain compulsive desires is, to that degree, also lacking in personal freedom or autonomy. The question remains, however, as to what extent social pressures play a role in determining both her value system and her view of herself.

Michael Sandel (2012) argues that we have moved from being a society with a market economy to being a market society. This book argues that some members of our society have moved from being individuals who consume goods to being consumed by goods. The dizzying multiplication of new wants can, for some vulnerable individuals, become needs for more and more, a pattern that can consume their lives.

In chapter one, the question of what determines healthy acquisition from the unhealthy kind is covered, and the different symptoms of the specific disorders are delineated. The issue of internal compulsion or appetitive internal forces is seen as Freud's major revolutionary contribution to a new (and much more complex) theory of action and desire. The presentation and analysis of this important issue, in chapter 3, is more technical, and this chapter can be skipped by readers with only a general interest.

Trapped in a consumption pattern where coercion and desire correspond, the individual with pleonexia has a frozen behavior pattern of insatiable craving. John Maynard Keynes's 1930 utopian essay, "Economic Possibilities for our Grandchildren," is instructive in its error.[22] Keynes was right to see the disposition of pleonexia as a psychological malady. However, his prediction that, once capitalism had supplanted "the struggle for subsistence" workers would voluntarily reduce their hours to fifteen a week, increasing their time for leisure and cultural pursuits, ignored the insatiable nature of the drive to accumulate money and consumer objects. The habit of equating love with possessions, for all too many of us, begins at a very early age, and is reinforced by media and marketing. The diagnostic criteria of whether or not the individual understands the true value of the objects she buys or possesses has been used to distinguish hoarding from compulsive buying. It is argued here that this is not an accurate or even useful distinction to make.

The concluding chapter presents some recommendations for treatment of acquisitive disorders. If being able to temper ones acquisitive appetites is a positive disposition, one that leads to greater well-being, then the question of how one acquires this trait is central. It is shown that, just as the unhealthy disposition of pleonexia was recognized by ancient cultures, some of the therapeutic techniques they developed to encourage temperance can still be effective today and should be added to the treatment regimen. It is shown that a whole tool box of techniques is needed, in light of the recognition that the causes of these disorders are multiple and the cultural influences are so powerful. Therapeutic techniques used by self-help groups are seen to have been independently developed by ancient cultures. These early therapeutic approaches have the added benefit of providing theoretical explanations that take into consideration the significant role played by the imagination, as well as the social and political influences, while also giving insight as to why they were so effective. The therapist needs to transcend the traditional divisions between psychotherapeutic approaches if she wishes to help her client develop healthy consumer behavior.[23] The clinical approach advocated here is based on the evidence that emotions are "evaluative."[24] It also builds on the feminist group technique of consciousness-raising, thereby incorporating important new insights from social and cultural analysis.

CHAPTER I

The All-Consuming Self

I count him braver who
overcomes his desires than him
who conquers his enemies, for
the hardest victory is the victory
over self.
          —Aristotle

Things are in the saddle,
And ride mankind.
          —Emerson

Gloria had known Martha for a little over a year.
Although Martha was quite shy, they had shared some brief
conversations after services at their small, suburban,
congregation. Martha didn't have a car, and, eventually,
Gloria became her major source of getting to church events.
From time to time, Gloria wondered why it was that Martha
always insisted that she be picked up in front of her house;
but, she chocked it up to Martha's obvious difficulty
establishing intimacy. It was, therefore, a surprise when, after
services one Sunday, Martha mentioned that her house had

become "a bit untidy", and that she could use some assistance "sorting things out".

Martha took a long time opening her door. Gloria soon understood why, as it was not easy pushing the door all the way open. Gloria's first impression was of a sea of papers everywhere she looked. She was surprised to see so many shopping bags, and even more surprised to find that they were filled with multiple pairs of the same clothing; many of the items still had their original tags. Martha had always been neatly dressed, but Gloria never thought of her as very fashion conscious. As Gloria made her way, with difficulty, past the kitchen, she glanced, with horror, at the kitchen stove, which was also covered with papers and other combustible objects.

But, it was when the main object of her visit began that Gloria got her first inkling of the cause of all this clutter. Martha was willing to move things around, but she strongly resisted any suggestion that they discard, even the most trivial, item. As the time went by, Gloria and Martha became more and more frustrated with each other, but for different reasons. Gloria couldn't understand why Martha felt the need to have so many examples of the same blouse, especially when she hadn't even taken them out of the bag. Martha became increasingly upset that Gloria wasn't helping her, in the one way she agreed she needed assistance, the only thing she had asked for, which was sorting and arranging her things. The two women decided that they would try again another day.

Henry presented to a private mental health clinic, not far from his upscale suburban neighborhood. He admitted that he was only there because his wife had "laid down the law" regarding his excessive spending. Initially, he attributed his problem to the recent downturn in the housing market, as the company he worked for as a salesman depended on the robust construction notable in his state. He admitted to getting used to "living well", as the fruits of his hard work and excellent selling skills. He was angry that his wife, who he felt benefited equally from his efforts, was now insisting he had a mental health problem. It soon became apparent that the things he spent so lavishly on, tools and sports equipment, were really items his wife never utilized or desired. It was only after the therapist insisted on a couples meeting, however, that the full extent of Henry's problem behavior was understood. Not only did he have eight credit cards, repeatedly taking out new ones to pay off old balances; but, most significantly, he recently had started skipping mortgage payments on their new house, putting the couple at risk of foreclosure. Eventually, Henry admitted that he had a problem resisting sales, and that his basement and shed were filling up with equipment he no longer had the time to use. He admitted that he was ashamed at behavior that placed all he valued in jeopardy, including the house he had always dreamed about owning.

In his individual sessions, Henry told of parents who would buy him more and more toys, but never seemed to have the time to spend with him that he most desired. He came to see that he equated the possessions he purchased with his own sense of success and personal fulfillment. With the help of some credit counseling, and more couples sessions, he eventually regained some security in his marriage and life.

Martha and Henry suffer from different examples of what has come to be called "consumer pathologies."[1] Voltaire wrote that "there are no true pleasures without true needs."[2] A determining symptom in distinguishing between different types of pathological consumption behaviors is whether objects are truly desired for their intrinsic value, perceived need, or distorted value. The awareness that desires are endless and insatiable has been a principle of religious and philosophical wisdom for millennia. The role that the abstract nature of money plays in this insatiability was described at least as early as Schopenhauer.[3] Some have argued that it is an essential part of human nature that we are never satisfied with anything. The extent to which this view is a reflection of the great transformation of western culture will be examined in the next chapter. The knowledge that

27

some ancient Mayans gambled to the point of causing serious harm to their family lends credence to the universal nature of some addictions.[4] Goethe summed up this aspect of human nature in one line: "For man must strive, and striving he must err." Certainly, it is the case that our acts of consumption rarely live up to our full expectations.[5] The fact that the accumulation of money and consumer objects has a tendency to become emotionally all-encompassing is a defining feature of behavioral addictions. This feature is mirrored, on a social level, by a growing tendency for capitalist values to replace the values once associated with every area of social interaction, from the family to sporting events.[6]

The kind of personal, familial, and social distress and harm experienced by Martha and Henry is a defining feature of behavioral or what has been called *process* addiction, along with their failure to restrain or change their actions, even when aware of such negative consequences.[7] An important distinction with hoarding behavior is that this distress is strongly aroused by the discarding of objects.

It is important to note that the consumer products are not the cause, in the sense of being necessary and sufficient, of the addictive behavior. This is more apparent when it comes to process addictions, such as gambling, but it is equally true for substance dependence, where there are many instances of the use of the substance without "causing" an addiction.[8] It should not be surprising that a holistic approach is needed for understanding and treating such complex human behavior. For example, there are treatment implications for someone like Martha, in that, except in the totally restrictive environment of a monastery, shopping is a part of life. As is the case with certain eating disorders, total abstinence is not an option.[9] Clearing up this confusion puts the focus where it needs to be, on the motivational and thought processes of the individual, on contributing social factors, and on the underlining neurological mechanisms of the addictive behaviors. Again, this is particularly true for cases like Martha's. The myriad consumer goods that have been created and are produced by consumer capitalism have greatly improved the quality of our material life; in themselves, they are not the problem. However, as John Kenneth Galbraith pointed out, in his influential *The Affluent Society,* there is something problematic about praising our economy for satisfying our wants when it creates those same wants.[10] Therefore, focusing on the individual and society inevitably involves consideration of personal and social values.[11] On the one hand, the reluctance of the psychiatric community to raise such issues is totally understandable, given the unfortunate history of judgmental abuse in the field. On the other hand, most, if not all, of the diagnostic criteria used by the mental health profession are saturated with value terms, such as 'excessive,' 'normative,' 'social harm,' and 'actual value.' One reason that these value concepts have become necessary, at least when it comes to addictions, is because of the well-documented fact that, even in the case of chemical addiction, there is no one to one correspondence between the amount of consumption and dependency, some light consumers have problems and some heavy consumers do not. It has become necessary, therefore, to add diagnostic criteria of long-term negative sociocultural consequences of the behavior. Also, the failures of behavioral psychology have taught us that there is really no way to think about actual practice without taking into consideration a person's beliefs and our own value judgments. What we believe has a direct impact on how we behave; and it also has a direct impact on any scientific investigation. But, just as there is no one thing that we all must believe, so there is no one way that all people should behave. The way around this dilemma is the concept of *subjective well-being*, developed in the concluding chapter. As we will see, this concept allows for a liberal theory of human flourishing that can be applied to a pluralist society, without imposing a rigid formula.

Another conceptual problem that needs to be addressed, early on, is the many different terms that have been used to designate problematic consumer behavior.[12] The pioneering German psychiatrist, Emil Kraepelin, described a syndrome he labeled "oniomania" (literally, "buying mania") in 1915, that later found its way into Eugen Bleuler's highly influential *Textbook of Psychiatry* (1924), in a general category that included kleptomania and pyromania. Other labels that have been used are: 'impulse buying and spending,' 'compulsive buying,' 'compulsive shopping,' 'shopping addiction,' and the least useful, 'shopaholic.' This profusion of labels mirrors a more general conceptual confusion between the concepts of impulsiveness, compulsiveness, addiction, and dependency. There have been disagreements about how to define, understand, and measure all of these terms. The role of habitual styles of cognitive processing is clearly a key to understanding these mental concepts. Forethought, for example, is a central component in most definitions of impulsivity.[13] The ability to make a decision about the personal value of an object, in a reasonable amount of time, has been identified as a key component of many individuals like Henry.[14] The earliest literature emphasized the impulsive nature of shopping and spending disorders. A compulsion, under this usage, is defined as an irresistible impulse. However, impulsivity is made up of a wide number of separate cognitive tendencies, including: a fixation on the present, a constant search for novelty, intense experiences, and excitement, inability to restrain instinctual drives, and an inability to plan ahead.[15] What's more, there is evidence that different components of this cognitive/behavioral mix appear to be more prominent in certain individuals and in specific disorders.

Attention has been given to the developmental and familial influences contributing to these problems in cognition and behavior. However, even those researchers who have taken a more comprehensive, biopsychosocial approach have tended to ignore the cultural contribution to their development.[16] These cultural influences have taken advantage of the, perhaps universal and adaptive, human tendency to discount future rewards in favor of more immediate satisfaction.[17] One of the earliest physicians to discuss alcoholism, Benjamin Rush, a signer of the *Declaration of Independence*, recognized the loss of control, calling it a "palsy of the will."[18] This old idea that addiction could be explained as an instance of weakness of will has given way to a much more nuanced understanding of the relation of emotion and cognition. The early experiments by Walter Mischel and others on self-control in children and adults showed the importance of "temporal discounting," the fact that we tend to discount the reality of future rewards and consequences. The first experiments were, misleadingly, referred to as "the marshmallow test," because some involved creating a conflict in a child between accepting the smaller reward in front of them, or delaying in order to get a larger reward, such as two marshmallows. This bird in the hand strategy has been aptly termed "the hot-cold empathy gap."[19] It is one reason why cognitive strategies, such as distraction and delay, work in children and adults. It is easy to see how it could be practical and adaptive for our pre-civilized ancestors to grab what they can, when they can. But this tendency becomes a major problem in our society of abundance, with such wonderful tools as television, the internet and credit cards to greatly reduce the time and effort involved in acquisition. Many psychologists and marketing experts have called attention to the growing problem caused by temporal proximity, now that a purchase can be made, in the comfort of your home, with only a click of one's finger. An obvious conflict exits in our society, between strategies that adults have learned to resist temptation, and the motivation that companies devise to circumvent such control, in order to increase sales.

Important experiments conducted by Dennis Rook and Robert Fisher (1995) demonstrated the important role that our normative values play in how we will react to this cultural conflict. They note that over a third of people in the United States self-identify as impulsive buyers. They define this "trait" as "a consumer's tendency to buy spontaneously, unreflectively, immediately, and kinetically."[20] Their experiments were designed to determine the extent to which normative judgments about impulsive behavior play a role in whether or not individuals with this tendency tend to act on their impulses. Through most of recorded history, impulsiveness, like materialism, has had a bad press. It has been contrasted with those deliberative capacities that make one a responsible, rational, and caring agent. There is plenty of evidence indicating that cultural norms can either constrain or encourage certain behaviors. Rook and Fisher call attention to the complexity of this interaction between our impulses to act and our normative judgments about such action; they note, for instance, how ambivalence or conflict can act to heighten the aroused desire to purchase an item. In other cases we simply ignore the normative constraint, or create rationalizations for our actions. However, when the norms of a culture work to encourage impulsive behavior, as they increasingly do in consumer driven economies, this can lead to a disposition to perform impulsive spending behavior.

This fact that we tend to give greater salience to immediate rewards is, also, an old idea that has received confirmation from modern experiments. In Plato's dialogue, *Protagoras,* Socrates draws a useful analogy with visual experience, noting that objects closer to an individual look larger than those further away from us, just as we misjudge the rewards in front of us to be greater than those more distant. Alexander Hamilton, in *The Federalist Papers,* applied this more directly to our concerns when he noted that "immediate interests have a more active and imperious control over human conduct than general or remote considerations."[21] In contemporary theories of self-regulation, this is referred to as the problem of both physical and temporal proximity.[22] For physical proximity, think of the many different ways in which our immediate sensations are aroused when we walk into a modern department store or mall. The strategy of distraction or delay, used to counter this tendency, may help the child to keep her from grabbing the marshmallow in front of her, but for adults, who presumably have a hierarchy of values and motives, focusing on higher-order life goals, such as ones health or relationships may be more effective.[23] However, what can counter the strategy of delay, especially for adults, is the fear that the object desired may not be available, or, at least, not at this price, in the future; a fear that marketers can take advantage of in multiple ways. In other words, our very ability to abstract from our current situation to encompass broader ideas, values, and goals, what sets us humans apart, can also work against our ability to control our actions. However, given the well-established fact that positive reinforcements are more effective than negative, a more effective strategy can be promising oneself a future reward for avoiding an immediate temptation to buy. But being in a positive mood can actually impede self-regulation, since studies show that most people are at greatest risk for impulsive acts, such as buying, when they are feeling good; although a significant minority appear to be attempting to sooth a negative mood.[24] Ronald Faber and Kathleen Vohs report evidence that most people have only a limited capacity for self-control, placing us at greatest risk for impulsive purchases after an episode of previous resistance or when we are tired.[25] But, arguably the most salient fact is that, when any individual is in pain, especially emotional pain, immediate relief becomes the most urgent and insistent motivator.[26]

As if our myopic tendency to discount the future wasn't bad enough, an allied human cognitive propensity, called *affective forecasting*, has been identified. Why would anyone who knows the addictive power of a drug like nicotine, and the health effects of smoking, ever start smoking? One answer often heard is: I didn't think it would ever happen to me. The psychologists, Timothy Wilson and Daniel Gilbert (2005), performed experiments that showed that we all tend to have an "impact bias" when making predictions about our emotional reaction to future events, which effects our decision about our actions. We tend to overvalue the pleasure that a purchase will bring, and to undervalue the negative consequences of the debt. Psychological experiments have demonstrated that we engage in harmful and wasteful behavior because we prize our immediate pleasures more than our future well-being. [27]

Just like the alcoholic who picks up a drink while pledging to quit tomorrow, we spend in the present and vow to save in the future. We are just not very good at predicting our future wants or what we think we will need, a fact that Gilbert and Wilson label "miswanting." A number of reasons for this human weakness have been identified. For one thing, we all tend to focus on the single event or object in front of us, rather than on our general life circumstances or long term consequences, a cognitive bias that Daniel Kahneman calls the "focusing illusion," a bias summarized with this observation: "nothing in life is as important as you think it is when you are thinking about it."[28]

These research results are important for all economic activity, but they have a special application for an understanding of compulsive acquisition and hoarding. The economist and psychologist, George Loewenstein, has shown how they can be applied to addictive behavior, especially in market behavior.[29] We all know that it is not a great idea to go grocery shopping when we are hungry.

Loewenstein developed his theory based on such drive states as hunger, sexual desire, moods and emotions, and various cravings, grouped under the category of "visceral factors." Visceral, for Loewenstein, clearly means much more than what we normally associate with feelings.[30] His theory helps to explain the phenomenon of *affective forecasting*, by noting that when we are in a cold state, we are not good at predicting how we will react when we are later in a hot visceral state (his theory has been referred to as cold-to-hot empathy gaps). What is involved, in part, is what Loewenstein calls a "projection bias," whereby we tend to project our present feeling state into the future. Of course, this can work both ways, in that people in a hot state have difficulty predicting how they might react when they no longer experience their intense visceral reaction.

This model for addictive behavior seems most appropriate for addiction to drugs. Alcohol dependents often feel that they will be able to go to a party, or even to a bar, and will resist picking up a drink, only to suffer the negative consequences of their optimism. This is similar to the confidence, prevalent especially in America, with our strong individualist faith, that we can resist the negative influence of the people we hang around with. We are, the research demonstrates, viscerally attached to our cognitive biases. What Daniel Kahneman (2011) calls System 1, our immediate responses, rule our behavior, at least most of the time Loewenstein, however, applies his theory directly to shopping behavior, noting that marketers and sales people have learned to utilize visceral factors in their effort to manipulate our shopping behavior. He also makes an indirect argument for application of his theory to problems with shopping and spending, noting research showing that certain psychotropic medications, such as fluoxetine have been shown to have some positive effect on compulsive buying, as well as drug addiction.[31] Loewenstein's model has the added virtue of helping to explain the well-known adverse effect of environmental and other cues on relapse, what he calls cue-conditioned craving.[32] The research of psychologists such as Gilbert, Wilson, Kahneman, Loewenstein, and countless others, has greatly expanded our understanding of how our beliefs about ourselves and others are strongly influenced by our emotions, visceral factors, imaginations, and cognitive biases, only confirming the early insights of Hellenistic philosophers.

George Ainslie's work builds on these findings about impulsive behavior and applies them further to other issues in addictions; it will play an important role in my concluding chapter on treatment strategies. Suffice it to point out here that an obvious reinforcement of this human tendency to fail to accurately predict our future behavior that can influence the development of compulsive spending is through the use credit cards and similar devices. The disposition to be impulsive occurs in individuals who appear to lack the cognitive delay mechanism that protects others from acting on this universal tendency to want to gratify immediate desires. The fact that we can all identify with the concept of retail therapy (known as self-gifting in research on self-regulation) shows an intuitive understanding of the close relationship between feeling bad and poor impulse control. Also, losing some weight in order to be able to purchase a garment, for example, can work as a self-control strategy. But, self-gifting as a long range reward for resisting an immediate temptation is a dangerous habit to develop, given our constant bombardment by temptations and the many stresses in modern life.[33] This danger is increased, in our culture, where so-called normal shoppers are more likely to make an impulsive purchase to help relieve emotional distress; a tendency that has been proven by controlled experiments.[34] Studies have shown that, for some types of products, impulse buying accounts for an amazing 80% of purchases in the United States.[35] Self-gifting, of course, can be in the form of doing something we enjoy, rather than making a purchase. However, in a culture where activities often cost lots of money, even this way of controlling impulses can lead to a pattern of overspending and debt.

However, the motivating factors here are even more complicated. Most of us can relate to research that shows that a strong influence on much impulse buying comes from anticipated future regret. We buy something because it is on sale or we think it is rare, and we just know that we will have to live with long-term regret if we fail to yield to temptation now. This phenomenon has been labeled *hyperopia* in order to contrast it with myopic or short-term guilt or regret.[36] The short-term regret approach is focused on guilt reduction, increasing self-control and responsible behavior. The fact that compulsive buying engenders feelings of guilt and regret, leading to a closed, self-reinforcing, feedback loop has been well documented.[37] As David Krueger points out, the awareness, on some level, that one has purchased more than one needs or can afford, often leads to such negative judgments and emotions. He gives the example of a parent spending the money needed for his child's medicine.[38] Keinan and Kivetz argue that this traditional focus on "myopic regret" ignores the fact that people who are consistently prudent and resist hedonistic desires often live a life of deep regret at "missing out" on life's pleasures. It is particularly interesting that they note that individuals with low self-esteem are particularly vulnerable to such long-term regret. They point out that their research, at the very least, modifies the addiction theories about the effects of our tendency to discount the future, which are, perhaps, overly cognitive in their focus. They outline the obvious practical implications of their research, for advertising and marketing, for example lottery advertising that would play on fears of losing out on life's pleasures. They note that their research modifies, and does not replace, the findings about short-term regret, in that the same motivations can do battle in an individual psyche, in what they call "self-control dilemmas." There is strong evidence that regret from a loss is a more powerful emotion than the pleasure we get from a gain.[39] Therefore, a person who feels that he or she was deprived of love, and who equates receiving personal possessions with an act of love, would be at greater risk of developing compulsive buying.

What is so fascinating about these arguments is the degree to which they assume the materialistic values of our society as given, contrasting these values with a "self-righteous" Puritanism. They mention Plato and Aristotle in passing.[40] But the Greek concept of pleonexia attacks the whole idea that a person can live a good life through the acquisition and accumulation of material goods as irrational. In fact, Aristotle suggests yet another motivation behind such unlimited accumulation of material goods, namely, the irrational belief that it will somehow prolong our life.[41]

1.1 Compulsive Buying

A large number of investigators have stressed the intrusive and chronic aspect of compulsive buying, as well as the many quality of life problems that result, especially with relationships, finances, as well as legal issues.[42] People differ considerably in their ability to control or regulate their behavior. Also, a number of factors can influence an individual's capacity at self-regulation, including emotions, beliefs, relationships, and even energy level. Many other studies have shown the relationship between compulsive buying and other disorders, including substance abuse, anxiety, and depression, and self-calming or self-medicating effects of shopping episodes.[43] A major criterion suggested for the distinction between impulse control problems, compulsion and addiction has been the motivating factors involved, with the former disorders seen as driven by the need to relieve distressing affect, such as anxiety, while addictive behavior is driven by a desire for intense pleasure. However, most people appear to make impulsive purchases when they are in a positive mood, whereas compulsive buyers most often report a negative mood both prior and after purchasing, with the lift in mood occurring only during the buying episode.[44] Therefore, a more reliable distinction between impulsive and compulsive buying can be drawn using the notion of a complete breakdown in a person's capacity for utilizing self-regulation strategies.[45]

When I first suggested diagnostic criteria for compulsive buying and spending problems in the late 1980s, I compared them to impulse control and eating disorders.[46] The edition of the *Diagnostic and Statistical Manuel of Mental Disorders,* at that time, listed five specific disorders under their catch-all grouping of other impulse problems: Intermittent Explosive Disorder, Kleptomania, Pathological Gambling, Pyromania, and Trichotillomania (hair-pulling disorder). As usual, the impulsive behavior had to lead to some harmful outcome.[47] They added that the individual might not have planned to act as he/she did, or even been consciously aware of the impulse to behave in that fashion. I was critical of diagnostic labeling and the reification involved, and the lack of a consideration of social and cultural context. The latest edition of the *DSM* does have a lot more to say about the importance of cultural factors in diagnosis. However, the emphasis is clearly uncritical. A critical therapeutic approach would note the irony that a strong motivation behind such instrumental labeling is the important role it plays in selling services and medications.

A growing body of evidence has shown that behavioral addictions can activate the very same parts of the brain involved in reward that have been associated with drug dependence. The degree of impairment plays an essential role in determining compulsive behavior. But, it is the discovery of neurological mechanisms, even more than the craving for intense pleasure, which has become the distinguishing characteristic that moves a disorder into the addiction category. The authors note that the jury is still out concerning similar neurological mechanisms for other, so-called, behavioral addictions. Recent studies using functional MRI machines and other tools have suggested similar reward stimulation results with compulsive buyers.[48] There is evidence that most people shop impulsively when they are in a positive mood.[49] Compulsive behavior, on the other hand, is most often associated with relief from a negative mood, as well as a high incidence of negative consequences.[50] The role that the frontal cortex plays in making decisions about the long-term consequences of our decisions has been well documented. In addition, there is evidence that the behavioral addictions have the same magnifying effect on the secretion of dopamine and on its receptors in the brain that have been found to play a central role in drug addiction.[51] There is suggestive evidence that the neural mechanism that helps with impulse control, situated in the prefrontal cortex, is eventually damaged by the increased production of dopamine, making it even harder to break the cycle of addictive behavior. The neurotransmitter serotonin has been associated both with the experience of craving and with compulsive buying behavior.[52] Whether or not compulsive buyers also develop tolerance and withdrawal has yet to be proven. Meanwhile, a whole new approach to marketing, called neuromarketing, has developed, with alarming implications for freedom. On the other hand, at least as far back as Plato and Aristotle, philosophers were aware the power of our bodily desires to overwhelm our behavior, our freedom, and a person's understanding of what nurtures personal well-being. It is for that reason that Aristotle argued that a major function of a good government was, not just to educate the citizen about what behaviors promote a flourishing life, but also to help the individual to develop a disposition to restrain the body.

Individuals with kleptomania, like compulsive buyers, usually do not value the objects they acquire, finding their pleasure or relief in the process or behavior itself. The fact that it is often not the material object or commodity simpliciter that is the end of desire, at the very least, complicates any manipulationist causal explanation for these disorders. Any theory about the external compulsion to possess the object must include the symbolic value ownership conveys or represents for many individuals in our society. In these disorders, the psychological coercion of the exchange process is greater than simply desiring objects or commodities. For example, the sense of increased self-worth and power that can come from spending large sums of money can be very seductive and is part of the "high" that comes from the shopping experience.[53] The fact that this high is followed by a crash when the bills come due is an example of the emotional feedback loop so common in addiction. Of course, shopping binges or episodes can just as often be accompanied by feelings of anxiousness, helplessness, guilt and even panic, as they are by excitement or euphoria.[54] This emotional and symbolic value component of the process is also one reason why there is a growing preoccupation with shopping and an extensive fantasy life which revolves around the ownership of commodities.[55] This preoccupation, as well as the urge or impulse, plus the behavior itself, all increase substantially during periods of disturbed mood, especially feelings of depression, depletion or inner emptiness and tension.[56] This fantasy aspect is important for a true understanding of psychological freedom and autonomy, defining wealth in human and interpersonal terms, something critical for the treatment of consumer disorders.

I based the model of consumer disorders that I developed in the 1980s on some pioneering studies of eating disorders, especially the excellent feminist approach of Susan Bordo, as well as the comprehensive, multidimensional analysis of Garfinkel and Garner (1982).[57] The diagnostic criteria that I developed at that time are still applicable today. The essential features of compulsive buying are: a persistent failure to resist temptation to shop or otherwise acquire commodities, which behavior compromises, disrupts, or damages, personal, family, financial, or vocational pursuits. I argued that consumer disorders were best understood using the "dispositional disorders" model of Stanton Peele, and the "lifestyle trait" model of impulsive buying by Dennis Rook, which is long-lasting and shows a slow progression.[58] These approaches had the advantage that they were contextualist, taking into consideration the social and cultural influences that contribute to the development of the disorder. I, also, noted that compulsive buying most often occurs in a pattern of spontaneous or impetuous acts, such as buying sprees.[59]

The kinds of problems that arise with compulsive buying and spending include: defaulting on debts, often including mortgages and multiple credit cards; disrupted family relationships; increased disapproval from significant others; and a number of antisocial behaviors (including, shoplifting, borrowing from illegal sources, forgery, embezzlement, fraud, and tax evasion — any criminal behavior, however, is typically nonviolent). There is often restlessness and irritability if, as a result of these problems, the compulsive buyer is unable to shop or spend money.

A large number of researchers have pointed out that people who suffer from compulsive spending and buying score high on tests of materialistic values, image consciousness, and external validation. These individuals believe that their stuff will provide them some positive emotional return. It is for this reason that focusing only on the stuff can cause one to miss the underlying cause. In fact, these very same individuals score high on measures of low self-esteem, feelings of inadequacy, and personal emptiness. As one person put it, her purchases were her "passport to popularity."[60] Martha Nussbaum reminds us of "the especially complex thoughts that humans are likely to form about their own need for objects, and about their imperfect control over them."[61] Cognitive behavioral studies have noted that subjects diagnosed with compulsive buying disorder have difficulty distinguishing between their behavior and so-called normal buying.[62] A number of researchers have noted the importance of the symbolic power of commodities, and related this to issues of personal identity and ego strength.[63] Countless advertisements encourage us to believe that we can enhance our image, our social standing, and our sense of personal fulfillment simply by purchasing their product. We will see in Chapter 2 that any one-sided manipulation thesis is too simple if it fails to take into consideration this complex dance between real and imagined needs, between the intrapsychic dynamics of the buyer and the pressures brought by social and cultural norms. It is here that any weakness is created and exploited in the most vulnerable. This is another kind of feedback loop, which performs a complex pas de deux with the addiction loop described earlier. Restoring a healthy and flourishing life involves addressing issues in all these areas, including values and beliefs, as well as emotional needs and social pressures.

This is a good place to raise the issue of gender prevalence. Early studies of compulsive buying asserted that there was a much higher incidence of this disorder among women, hence the emphasis, especially in psychoanalytic studies, on shopping binges for clothing, on body image, and related narcissistic injury. The assumption is that, at least in our culture, women are more image conscious, and, therefore, more susceptible to manipulation by marketers (this assumption will be examined further in Chapter 2). A caveat was sometimes inserted, noting that women tended to seek psychotherapy much more often than men, thereby introducing a sampling error. Donald Black addressed this issue by noting that men tended to larger, more expensive, commodities, like electronic equipment.[64] This female gender prevalence has been questioned.[65] In his 2007 review of the literature on compulsive buying, Black noted a gender discrepancy in studies of prevalence in the disorder. In his 2011 study of the worldwide epidemiology of the disorder, he found a clear preponderance of female sufferers, along with an onset between adolescence and the early 20s, with the prevalence of the full disorder in people in their 40s. Studies of hoarding disorder show a similar age for onset, and only a slightly older age group for those in treatment.[66] Contrary to what we might expect, research does not confirm that those with hoarding disorder had an early history of material deprivation, but, rather they come from all socioeconomic backgrounds. However, those individuals with a large living space are better able to hide their problem from society. Like many problematic behaviors, consumer disorders most often start to increase slowly and only come to the attention of others when they are obviously out of control. In a study published the same year, only a slight greater prevalence in women was reported, 6.0 versus 5.5%.[67] Of course, any difference in numbers and gender could be explained by the different screening instruments used and their scoring, as well as any sampling issues. Whatever the facts are concerning gender factors, there appears to be strong evidence that the incidence of compulsive buying is increasing among the young.[68] It should not be surprising that the advent of credit cards and other forms of easy credit, television, especially the shopping channels, Groupon, internet shopping and other "advances" in technology have contributed greatly to this increased incidence of compulsive buying. The shopping channel is of particular interest, because of the techniques used to appeal directly to the, largely, female, and often lonely, audience.[69]

A personality trait commonly noted in both compulsive buyers and people with hoarding disorder is perfectionism.[70] The psychological concept of perfectionism is fraught with difficulties, not least because it has been associated with so many different disorders, but, even more importantly, because it is often associated with normal mental functioning. Therefore, an early distinction was drawn between so-called normal and neurotic perfectionism, with positive versus negative motivation as a primary distinguishing feature.[71] A failed effort to gain parental approval is often the source of this trait, but, it is also an example of the kind of alienation of personal worth that Rousseau and other critics hold comes from the desire for recognition through material possessions.

Although as many as two thirds of individuals who suffer from hoarding disorder also have symptoms of compulsive buying, a significant percentage of people with hoarding problems have a much broader problem with acquisition, and the two disorders should not be conflated.[72] There are, after all, other ways of acquiring things besides shopping; just try not discarding your mail for a month and see how big a pile of papers you end up with. This points to the important distinction, namely that hoarding disorder is not as much a problem about acquisition as it is a problem with discarding things; an over attachment to inanimate objects or, in some cases, to animals. It has only been within the last decade that a muddle over terminology, concepts, and differential diagnosis has been cleared up enough to bring about the new diagnostic criteria for a separate category of hoarding disorder. It is to this new understanding that I will turn to in the next section.

Compulsive buying is thought of by psychiatry as one of a number of excessive behavioral patterns, such as gambling, and, in the newest diagnostic manual (*DSM-V*) it is mentioned after the substance-related addictions. The average person associates substance use with addiction and understands the destructive potential of drugs, such as heroin. Clinicians know that there are degrees of dependence and affliction with all these disorders. An added problem with behavioral addictions is that, whereas most of us can avoid heroin, there are some behaviors, such as eating, which we cannot avoid, and others, such as shopping, that are extremely hard to avoid. Some other behaviors, like gambling, have become increasingly more difficult to avoid, given their promotion by government and the media. The role of culture and the media in promoting excessive buying will be examined in the next chapter. Here we need to look more closely at the symptoms and diagnostic criteria that indicate a problem with buying, as well as the different levels of dependence associated with this behavior. It is important to keep in mind, however, that individuals with these behavioral problems often present with comorbid psychiatric disorders, including substance addiction, as well as mood disorders, such as anxiety and depression.[73]

O'Gwinn, for example, developed one of the first, and, arguably, most widely used screening tools for diagnosing consumers with problematic behavior.[74] As the moral philosopher, Amelie O. Rorty pointed out, "social institutions and economic systems encourage and foster the very actions that they also condemn."[75] Not surprisingly, a big part of the stated motivation of these consumer experts, in studying and identifying problematic behavior, is to understand the behaviors, motives, and emotions of consumers considered normal. In fairness to them, however, it should be added that another big motivation behind their research is social well-being. It is interesting to note that, in a consumer culture, the medicalization of consumption behaviors, with the exception of some with compulsive hoarding and compulsive spending, would not serve the same kind of Foucaultian power or disciplining functions of other mental health or sexual practices. Restricting consumption and desire is far from being a goal of the governing power structures. However, the very different motivation behind the research of these marketing and advertising experts should not take away from the insights into consumer behavior, including problematic buying, that they have contributed. One trivial outcome of this research is that supermarkets are now relabeling their personal products section with the trendy psychological term *well-being.*

The concept of well-being, as I use it here, which draws upon, the closely related, concepts of John Dewey's "the democratic way of life," John Stuart Mill's vision of healthy personal growth in *On Liberty*, and *The Subjection of Women,* as well as the "capabilities approach" of the Nobel laureate economist Amartya Sen, and the philosopher, Martha Nussbaum, is much more integral to human flourishing and freedom (there is room here for only the barest treatment of these rich ideas).[76] This emphasis on enhancing personal freedom and enabling capabilities can be defended against the critique of certain poststructualists that it is ahistorical and ethnocentric, but such a defense would take me too far afield.

But, what are the specific behavioral traits that distinguish compulsive buying from the conventional impulse buying that most individuals engage in, on a fairly regular basis? Is it just a matter of frequent impulses or urges to purchase objects one knows, on some level, you don't really need? An important finding of the consumer researchers is that compulsive aspect of buying is not really about the objects purchased, but rather motivated by the process of consumption itself.[77] We will see that this is a major distinction with most individuals with hoarding disorder, who usually overvalue the objects they collect.[78] However, the distinction is not hard and fast, as there are individuals with hoarding disorder who collect items and never take them out of their wrappings. In fact, there is a finer distinction to be made, in that hoarding appears to be more about ownership, than about the objects owned.[79] The fact that for most people in our culture conspicuous consumption fails to fulfill their fantasies, and, that "the actual act of consumption is often something of an anticlimax" has been noted many times.[80] It is to these distinct features of hoarding disorder that I must now turn.

1.2 Compulsive Hoarding

The art of our necessities is strange,
That can make vile things precious.
King Lear, Act 3, Scene 2

Hoarding, like compulsive buying, was originally seen as an impulse control disorder, with emphasis on the intrusive, uncontrollable nature of beliefs about possessions, similar to the cognitive pattern in obsessive compulsive disorder. The difference noted was in the nature of the beliefs, with compulsive buyers seeking relief from fears about failing to acquire possessions and individuals with compulsive hoarding fearing negative outcomes from discarding objects.[81] . Of course, as we have seen, the same individual can have both sets of fears and beliefs. Frost and Hartl identified three separate, but closely related, cognitive deficiencies in individuals with hoarding disorder: difficulties with processing information about their possessions; problems regulating their emotional reaction to possessions; and erroneous beliefs about their possessions (1996).

The neurologist Antonio Damasio has shown how information processing, our emotions, and our beliefs closely interact with and influence each other in ways that lead to relatively fixed patterns of behavior.[82] His somatic marker hypothesis has helped economists develop more realistic models of decision-making than the classical rational choice model, which explains the buying behavior of individuals as based on rational decisions about maximizing their gains. Compulsive buying, spending, and hoarding comprise behaviors that are very hard to explain using this classical economic model of rational consumers making rational choices or decisions about their spending. The old model assumed that individuals not only possess and act on knowledge about which purchases are the best for their price, but they also have self-awareness about which purchases make the most sense given their own needs and well-being. In fact, rational choice theory, the view that people calculate the costs and benefits of their action before proceeding, has been shown to be highly deficient as an explanation of normal economic behavior, as psychologists have taught economists about the many ways our decisions are irrationally motivated. This critique of a rationalist model of acquiring and hoarding will be examined in the next chapter. Suffice it to note here that Pierre Bourdieu's dispositional theory of consumption is a far richer model to explain the kind of behaviors being described here. Value judgments, and ideas about acquiring, saving, and discarding possessions, are at the center of the diagnostic assessment and treatment of hoarding disorder.

In an important survey article on the neurobiology of hoarding, Sanjaya Saxena adds to our understanding of these tendencies to fear negative outcomes from failing to acquire or from discarding possessions. He notes some other character traits more specifically found in those with hoarding disorder, namely "indecisiveness, perfectionism, procrastination, disorganization, and avoidance."[83] It is not hard to see how indecisiveness and disorganization can be a big component of hoarding, but it might seem counterintuitive that traits such as perfectionism and procrastination are strongly associated with this disorder. However, neurobiological evidence is mounting that areas of the brain involved in decision-making and emotional regulation are somehow impaired in individuals with compulsive hoarding. This research has the potential of eventually providing an explanation of how information processing deficits effect most individuals with compulsive hoarding.[84]

One of the factors that sets hoarding apart from some other disorders is the extent to which it can be seen as a community health problem.[85] Individuals with hoarding problems most often come to clinical attention because of referrals, many compulsory, from public health officials, housing authority inspectors, child protection officers, animal control, and other security officers, as well as fire inspectors. It is not unusual to encounter tenants who have gone through multiple evictions. Individuals with so-called late life hoarding often have had problems for years, but

70

they only come to the attention of others when they move into tighter quarters. Those with chronic illness may be unable to find their medications, their testing kit, or their walking aid. It is readily apparent from this list that hoarding is a public health problem that is underreported and treated. Furthermore, the involvement of the legal/regulatory system, especially when combined with the limited insight and denial of most individuals with hoarding disorder, often leads to an adversarial relationship with treatment providers, contributing to the high recidivism rate and family frustration. Most individuals with hoarding disorder are stuck in a precontemplation stage of change.[86] Years of family efforts to plead, cajole, threaten have only led to complex emotional reactions, such as shame, resentment, distrust, hurt, and defensiveness. Incidences of outright family rejection are high. It is for this reason that early detection and prevention, especially working with family members, primary care physicians, and educators, must be a major focus with hoarding disorder. Helping them to recognize the cognitive distortions and negative emotional reactions engendered by their prior coercive efforts can be critical to the kind of team effort needed to bring about positive change. Here again, understanding the social context of these disorders can reduce the tendency to stigmatize and blame. A major result of motivational interviewing is to help place the problem outside the individual who suffers from the disorder, lowering shame and guilt, while increasing competence, engagement, and personal autonomy. Focusing on higher level values, for example contact with a grandchild, can strengthen ambivalent emotions that assist in slowly bringing about positive change. This issue and related treatment recommendations will both be addressed more fully in the concluding chapter.

This public health aspect is especially true when dealing with a subset of people with hoarding disorder, namely those individuals who hoard animals. It has only been in the last decade or so that this particular group of people with hoarding problems has been studied, often as a result of sensational legal cases reported in the media. The demographics for this subset appear to have a higher representation of women, who live alone, and are elderly, with the number of animals reaching, in some cases, to as high as a hundred or more, often with some dead or close to dying.[87] Although a majority of people who hoard animals appear to fit the criteria for hoarding disorder, only a small percentage of individuals with hoarding disorder collect animals. A fascinating dichotomy in the motivation of people who hoard animals has been identified. The majority appear to be driven by a desire to rescue and care for these animals, which becomes overwhelming and irresistible. A smaller subset, however, appear to be uncaring, seeing the animals merely as possessions they can control. Both groups end up being abusive, but the latter usually cause the greatest harm to the animals.

The abusive nature of this behavior, its relative intractability, and the emotional reaction it engenders in the public all work against resolving this complex behavioral and social problem. Another complication is often encountered by animal control officers. Anyone who has had to enter the home of an animal hoarder can attest to the strong ammonia odor which is often present. There is growing evidence of the effects of ammonia toxicity on health, including mental status.

Early medical psychology used a wide variety of purely descriptive terms under the categories of 'mania,' 'phobia,' and 'dementia'.[88] Those individuals who had a problem with hoarding were labeled with terms such as collecting mania, bibliomania, or disposophobia. Bibliomania, for example, was described as "a pathological, irresistible mental compulsion" to collect books.[89] It should be noted that people with hoarding disorder often collect papers of all sorts, especially newspapers and magazines. The economist John Maynard Keynes provides an interesting example of, what he calls bibliomania, in his biographical essay on his colleague,

William Stanley Jevons. He notes that Jevons not only collected thousands of books, but also as many pamphlets, "lining the walls and passages of the house and packed in heaps in the attics," and how this became "an embarrassment" to his family after Jevons death.[90] Edward G. Winslow argues persuasively that Keynes was influenced by psychoanalytic theories, especially in his idea that we have an instinct to hoard objects.[91] The term syllogomania (literally, frenzied collecting) was usually applied to those who collect rubbish, and associated with the badly labeled Diogenes syndrome. This last named condition was applied to a smaller subset of mostly elderly patients who live under conditions of gross neglect and squalor, sometimes referred to as senile squalor.[92] These individuals tend to live in total isolation, sometimes with too many pets, and under conditions of extremely poor hygiene, often accompanied with a stubborn refusal to accept any help. The authors of a recent book on *Severe Domestic Squalor* provide some useful clarification for this, unhelpful, former terminology.[93] This clarification is important because these various categories of hoarding behavior point to different etiologies, which respond to specific treatment approaches.

Hoarding behaviors, such as Henry's, were long classified as just a clinical subgroup of behaviors under the categories of obsessive-compulsive disorder and obsessive-compulsive personality disorder. This is ironic given that many who suffer from this disorder prefer to refer to their things and to themselves using the euphemistic terms clutter and clutterer, words which, according to the *Oxford English Dictionary,* carry a strong connotation of disorder and mental and verbal confusion. The chosen name, for example, of the twelve-step, self-help groups is Clutterer's Anonymous. Their preferred use of these terms is doubly ironic given that most individuals with hoarding disorder appear to have a deficit in organizational functions, and the word hoard has long carried connotations of a treasure or a collection of valuables, which more closely fits what most people with hoarding disorder think of their stuff. However, the word hoarder has been negatively applied, since ancient times, to individuals who stored away commodities, such as grain, in order to drive up the market price. In their popular book on hoarding, Randy Frost and Gail Steketee describe a woman who is highly distressed when she focuses on her "clutter," but sees each individual item as "comforting" and valuable.[94] It should be noted that this woman is unusual in that most people with hoarding disorder fail to register any distress about their clutter, and most appear to not even notice it. Also, it should not be considered unusual that a clinical label, such as hoarder, tends to take on negative associations for those who are the object of such labeling. Meanwhile, there is some evidence that males who suffer from hoarding behavior prefer to call themselves collectors.

The value of the objects collected and hoarded, of course, is a subjective criterion, and yet it often figures directly in the diagnosis. There is growing evidence that hoarding disorder results from a pathological exaggeration of tendencies we all inherit. It is easy to see how a tendency

to hoard could have brought some evolutionary advantage

for our ancestors. There is evidence, for example, that we

all have some tendency to relate to objects we own as if

they were alive or an extension of our body, a behavior

carried to an extreme by many with hoarding disorder.

James Beggan (1992) gives the amusing example of a

tennis player getting angry at his racket. Experiments by

behavioral economists, for example, have identified what

they call an *endowment effect.*[95]. In a series of classic

experiments, behavioral economists demonstrated that we

have a clear tendency to place a higher subjective value on

objects we happen to possess than we place on an object of

the same objective value that we don't already own. This

was seen as an example of a more general, innate, aversion

to the loss of something we own; a reaction anyone can see

immediately when you try to take a toy away from a baby.

In normal adults, this effect is restricted primarily to objects

we not only own, but also utilize, as opposed to objects

clearly intended only for sale or trade.[96] In one of the most

often cited experiments, a random selection of half of the

subjects, called Sellers, were given especially attractive

coffee mugs, while the other subjects, referred to as Buyers,

were only allowed to look at their neighbor's mug. Both

groups were then asked to record the value of the mug.

Daniel Kahneman notes the "dramatic" results: "the

average selling price was about double the average buying

price, and the estimated number of trades was less than half

of the number predicted by standard theory."[97] The mere

fact of ownership significantly increases the value of an

object. Kahneman and Tversky determined that our general

tendency toward loss aversion means that we are not

willing to risk losing them, unless we have the chance to at

least double our winnings.[98] These findings have special

importance for understanding hoarding disorder. This is,

especially, true for elderly sufferers, referred to as late life

hoarders, who have experienced so many other losses in

their lives, such as loss of work, mobility, and social

relations. Many of these same elderly sufferers have other chronic conditions that can complicate their mental condition. It is no wonder that they should resist having their possessions removed from their residence!

The importance of the endowment effect and loss aversion for an understanding of hoarding disorder is highlighted in efforts to identify the neurological underpinnings of the disorder. The thought processing, especially the decision-making and pathological attachment to possessions, of individuals who suffer from hoarding disorder points to the involvement of a strong neurological mechanism. Research to date implicates an area of the frontal part of the limbic system, the anterior cingulate cortex, involved in feeling/emotion, executive attention, error-detection, and working memory. Because of its importance to emotion and cognition, Antonio Damasio has labeled this area the "fountainhead region."[99] Neuroimaging, epidemiological, and other studies have produced evidence that people who suffer from hoarding disorder have some kind of damage in this region.[100]

Another very interesting area that has been shown to be involved, in addition to the fountainhead region, is the insula cortex, an area deep within the cerebral cortex. The fact that the insula has also been implicated in visceral functions and the addictions lends credence to its importance in hoarding disorder. In one highly important set of experiments, subjects with symptoms of hoarding disorder showed reduced activity in these areas of their brains, than controls, when making decisions about objects that did not belong to them, but higher than normal activity when deciding about objects they owned.[101] In other words, their endowment effect was more pronounced, at least based on neural activity in these parts of the brain. Tolin and his colleagues note that a number of cognitive impairments that have been identified in subjects with hoarding disorder, such as problems with attention, recall, categorizing tasks, as well as the decision process are known to be focused in these cortical regions.[102] These identified areas of the brain normally function together to monitor our emotions, our risk taking, and to help us decide when and how to act. The proposed mechanism is one in which heightened emotional salience, specifically anxiety, is aroused by the decision to discard a possession, thereby leading to a paralyzing uncertainty. We all are aware than fears about the risks involved in making the wrong decision can keep us from acting in all kinds of situations. The physical evidence of hyperactivity in this system in the brain correlated with strong descriptive evidence of paralyzing indecisiveness in subjects with hoarding disorder. In addition to shedding some light on the mechanisms behind hoarding disorder, these neuropsychological studies of the degree of susceptibility to the endowment effect are also important for an understanding of compulsive acquisition. One major question is whether an individual has an enhanced attraction to items for possible acquisition, or an increased aversion to the loss of items they already own, or suffer from both emotional reactions.[103]

Recent studies of some people with hoarding problems, however, demonstrated that they show significant enough differences to warrant a separate category.[104] For example, one significant difference is that individuals with hoarding disorder often lack the anxiety about their behavior which is seen in most individuals with OCD. The latest edition of the *Diagnostic and Statistical Manual of Mental Disorders* standardizes these differences by listing hoarding as a separate disorder, but still under the general category of obsessive-compulsive disorders.[105]. They focus on the sufferer's extreme resistance to getting rid of objects, even when most individuals would consider them of little or no value. The individual's subjective need to retain the items, and her distress at parting with them, are additional criteria. The end result is what most people associate with hoarding, namely a living space so cluttered as to prevent its normal functions, for example, a bed with no room to sleep on it. A photographic rating scale, such as the Clutter Image Rating Scale is useful in diagnosing this key aspect.[106] As with other mental health disorders, the objective distress includes, not only problems with daily living, but significant impairment of relations, work, finances, and other social functions. The environmental dangers resulting from hoarding can best be seen in examples of piling papers, most often newspapers, next to a kitchen stove, that is also the only source of heating. The diagnostic criteria include the usual provisions that the behavior cannot be better explained by another disorder, such as major depression or dementia.

The degree of insight, if any, has proven to be especially important in the case of hoarding disorder. In a paper important for this book, Randy Frost, David Tolin, and Nicholas Maltby give a summary of the negative effects that this lack of insight has on treatment outcomes in cases of hoarding disorder (2010). The authors explore reasons for the very poor treatment outcomes for persons with hoarding as a primary diagnosis, as compared with obsessive compulsive disorder (OCD). The literature on hoarding is filled with stories of frustrated family, support, and treatment staff, with the high dropout rates, broken promises, treatment sabotage, and frequent relapse. As is the case with most addictive behavior, coercive methods have, at best, limited results, and most often are counterproductive. Frost, Tolin, and Maltby identify three different forms of poor insight: "*anosognosia* (lack of awareness of the existence of illness or its consequences), *overvalued ideation* (fixed and inflexible beliefs), or *defensiveness* (the use of denial and argument to resist influence by others)." Individuals in the first category are unlikely to present themselves for treatment, and usually only come to the attention of therapists through family intervention or some form of coercion. Not surprisingly, individuals with this lack of awareness have the poorest prognosis. Based on my many years of working with individuals coerced into treatment, I agree that the use of motivational interviewing is the most effective technique for slowly engendering some limited awareness with this difficult population.[107] This valuable approach is based on the fact that all of us, to a larger extent than we care to admit, create our own narrative of events. A central aspect of this approach is to identify the individual's core values and how these central goals are being circumvented by her overvaluation of her material possessions. Motivational interviewing has proven to be an effective way of dealing with the common defensive reaction generated whenever our self-defeating ideas and values are challenged. It is also based on an understanding of the self-reinforcing aspect of dependencies, as noted by Lawrence Lessig. These habitual behaviors may address certain needs, but they also create rewards that strengthen the habitual action and make these behaviors hard to resist.[108] Understanding this dynamic can help break through the defensiveness, which is the final aspect of poor insight identified by Frost, Tolin, and Maltby. Another related dynamic, which behavioral economists call *habituation,* is a common form of psychological adaptation whereby we get so accustomed to a new consumer object that we take it for granted and need more of it in order to achieve the same level of satisfaction. The economist Richard Layard borrowed the economic concept of the "hedonic treadmill," comparing it to the similar effect of tolerance in cases of alcohol and drug dependency. As Layard puts it, "you have to keep running in order for your happiness to stand still."[109] He provides evidence that this addictive pattern is most common with our material possessions, a fact well-known by advertisers who are required to nourish these behaviors.[110]

Historically, the term compulsion has been closely associated with the idea of coercion and external control. But psychologists, as we have seen, have long associated impulsivity with a lack of internal control, distinguishing compulsive behaviors by their repetitive nature and the highly value-laden concept of over-control.[111] Among those who prefer the label compulsive buying, the frequency and chronic nature of the behavior is used to distinguish it from impulse buying.[112] Cognitively, impulsiveness involves a lack of forethought, whereas compulsive behaviors are associated with an overabundance of thinking, a feature that leads to the pervasive character of these disorders, which literally take over all aspects of the sufferer's life. This capacity to co-opt an individual's thoughts and values means that strategies of delay and distraction are not effective tools, even when the individual may be able to apply them in other areas of her life. Jeanette Kennett makes this aspect the first distinction in her, very useful, three part definition of compulsion. She agrees with some others who have thought deeply about issues of agency and autonomy that what distinguishes a compulsive desire is that in these cases the usual methods of healthy self-control are ineffective. [113] However, she goes further to spell out what exactly this means. It does not mean that the individual is lacking in the means to act as she intends, though there are some phobias that can prevent action.

Rather, the strength of a compulsive desire is so great that it swamps all her other desires as well as her higher values. One strategy that is overcome is the ability to think of some other alternative action. A major goal of therapy should be to discover what aspects of this client's development and history go into making this particular action resistant to normal reasoning. It is here, also, where social and cultural forces should be taken into consideration. Kennett believes that the individual may still have the ability to prevent acting on her desire before it takes over her being; what she calls techniques of "diachronic self-control."[114] However, it is here, I wish to argue, that the idea of stages of addiction is a helpful one. At some advanced stages of addiction, as noted above, a person's whole being can be co-opted by the disorder. This tendency to encompass a person's being is, especially, prevalent in addictions of consumption, in light of the insatiable nature of material desire, a fact noted in all ages and by most cultures. It is this persistent aspect of behavior that is a distinguishing feature of hoarding disorder. The fact that items hoarded are often still packaged or have sales tags on them, something also noted in the case of compulsive buyers, is added evidence of their mood regulating function. There is strong evidence for the role of problems with beliefs, memory function, and other cognitive deficits in common failures in such self-regulatory behavior.[115]

The concept of *addiction* has been closely tied to the neurological mechanism of a reward system, with the ingestion of substances as the paradigm behavior. It is, also, tied closely with the concept of levels of dependency, with physical dependency, as manifested primarily by withdrawal symptoms, as the paradigm.[116] Gary Watson (1999) has drawn an important distinction between being "overpowered," and being "seduced." Being overpowered, with its mechanistic and deterministic connotations, borrows too heavily from the concept of external coercion. Compulsion, in the sense of being forced to act in a certain way or not being free to perform an action one wishes, should be distinguished from what happens when a person acts contrary to her stated desire to refrain from shopping. Drug dependency is most often seen as resulting from the drugs ability to subvert the users will entirely. Individuals with behavioral addictions, however, often report that they feel pressured or coerced, not by the object, but by the need to relieve internal tension or anxiety that they feel can only be done by engaging in the compulsive behavior. The locus of control is, therefore, placed in the self. This distinction is an important one for deciding which treatment approach will be most likely to work, as well as for the social and political implications for the preventions of addictions. For example, a person's beliefs about a certain object or reward have been shown to play an important role in their ability to control their own behavior. As for the disease or medical model: until the recent advent of preventive medicine and epidemiology, illnesses were held to be almost entirely involuntary afflictions by modern medical science. Nicotine addiction, to take the most obvious example, certainly blurs any hard and fast

distinction between a mechanical/deterministic explanation

and one based on voluntary behavior.[117] It is important to

add that individuals who suffer from compulsive buying

and spending report the same increased mood arousal

acknowledged in substance addictions, feelings of being

high or getting "a rush" when they buy or spend.[118] The

fact that these elevated mood states are temporary, and that

they lead to behaviors that exacerbate the problems

associated with negative mood states has been well

documented.

Psychologists and others trying to understand

addictive behaviors have found the philosopher Harry

Frankfurt's theory of what he calls "second-order desires"

very useful. Frankfurt (1988) argued that what

distinguishes humans from other animals is that we are

capable of forming desires about our desires. Frankfurt,

himself, used the well-known phenomenon of persons who

express a sincere desire to not indulge in taking drugs, but do so anyway, as a classic example of his theory. Therapists are very familiar with the many mixed motives which characterize human behavior, finding the symbol of pealing the layers of an onion as a useful picture. But, what seems to distinguish the kind of desires associated with addictive behavior, from other conflicting desires is their compelling nature or driven and repetitive quality. In this sense they are very much like the compulsion to constantly check things or wash ones hands. But, how useful is it to compare them to actions done under duress, for example at the point of a gun. On the other hand, this use of compulsion does help to explain the well-known influence of context, environment, and visual and other cues in relapse, something that is especially important in our consumer culture, where we are constantly bombarded with advertising.

At this point, Olav Gjelsvik (1999) adds a useful distinction, between freedom to act and freedom of will. A person may be free to buy this particular dress, let us say, even when she is acting contrary to her second order desire to stop her shopping addiction, which she recognizes is "out of control" and causing her no end of problems. Of course, many people with addiction do not have any second order desire to quit, but many do, and this is one way to help explain relapse and the type of compulsion we are dealing with. One group of investigators have borrowed a theory from economics, rational choice theory, to argue that each particular incident of buying, for example, can be seen as rational behavior, even though, in the long run, it leads to suffering and self-destruction.[119] This idea is useful in helping to identify any cognitive deficits that play a role in placing someone at risk for developing problematic consumer behaviors. Some individuals not only have deficits in their ability to form second order desires, but also in their ability to restrain or modify their own future behavior, such as by deciding to leave money and credit cards at home. Such a strategy is an example of what Jon Elster (1979) calls "self-binding."

Another way of looking at the compulsive nature of spending and shopping is to use the model of a closed feedback loop. This follows from research reported by Tim Kasser which shows that people who score high indicators of having a materialistic value system also score high for measures of low self-esteem. All indications are that their drive to accumulate wealth and possessions is fueled by their sense of inadequacy. Kasser reports other studies that show that individuals who share this value system spend more time watching television and looking at magazines that generate an unrealizable ideal of glamour and success, which generates what he calls "discrepancies" between their reality and the images promoted. These discrepancies only reinforce their sense of low self worth, leading to a "vicious circle," or what I've called a feedback loop, a process summarized by Goethe's *Faust*: "From desire we rush to satisfaction, but from satisfaction we leap to desire."[120] This model fits other addictive behavior patterns; think, for example, of the gambler who is always chasing his loses, or of the phenomenon of increased tolerance. This pattern of behavior fits with ancient wisdom about pleonexia and the insatiable nature of desire, as there is never enough money or things to fill up the vacuum inside. Each level of achievement only raises the bar further, and, as Kasser notes, becomes "the new norm" to measure one's self against. It also nicely captures the connection between repetition and compulsion, which has been recognized as a feature of mental disorders at least as far back as Freud. The close relationship between negative affect and events and impulse buying can easily lead to development of an addictive pattern. The social factors reinforcing this loop have been demonstrated experimentally.[121] Engaging in addictive behaviors leads to problematic outcomes that only reinforce guilt, anxiety, and low self-esteem reinforcing further use of substances and behaviors that provide temporary relief in a seemingly endless feedback loop.[122] However, as we will see, there is evidence that at least some individuals with hoarding problems do not fit so neatly into this pattern.

But before we turn directly to an examination of problematic consumer behavior patterns, there is one more conceptual issue that needs to be mentioned. There is a general tendency in science, in fact, in all intellectual endeavors, to "carve up nature" into discrete patterns and to label them as concrete entities. It is not necessary to get into the philosophical thickets surrounding issues of psychological taxonomy here.[123] However, this is especially an issue in psychiatry, personality theory, and, most importantly for us, behavioral addiction. Briefly, the issue is whether or not a system of diagnoses based on a cluster of observable signs and symptoms, with a predictable course and outcome can correctly differentiate between habitual behavior and pathological disorder. The criticism of the descriptive approach has come from those who argue that we need to understand the underlying causal and, specifically, cognitive/neurological mechanisms if we are to differentiate useful diagnostic categories.[124]

However, this criterion fails for, at least, two reasons: its realist requirement is too stringent for medical science. A full exposition of this argument would take us too far into the history and philosophy of science. Fortunately, it is not necessary, in light of the second reason, namely, that the diagnosis of compulsive buying, spending, and hoarding based on signs and symptoms has proved instrumental in identifying specific cognitive deficits associated with the different disorders. Furthermore, such information is already proving useful in identifying possible neurological causes for these disorders.

But, before taking a close look at these symptom clusters for consumer disorders, it is important to understand the cultural context that encourages and nourishes these unhealthy behaviors.

Chapter 2: The All-Consuming Society

Still pangs for gold the millionaire,
He's never done.
To many Fortune gives too large a share,
Enough to none.
— Martial

The most characteristic quality of
modern man; the strange contrast
between an inner life to which nothing
outward corresponds, and an outward
existence unrelated to what is within. It
is a contrast unknown to the Greeks.
—Nietzsche

In 1913 Freud wrote about the "powerful sexual factors"

which are involved in the value set upon money, and he noted "that

money questions will be treated by cultured people in the same

manner as sexual matters, with the same inconsistency,

prudishness and hypocrisy."[1] Over a hundred years later, the very

kind of reticence to discuss the role money plays in pathological

behaviors which Freud called attention to seems to have infected his

own creation. Despite Freud's own keen interest in the role of

money in character development, and the many articles of his immediate followers, recent theorists of psychoanalysis have remained virtually silent on subjects relating to money (an interesting exception to this generalization is the question of client fees). This silence is all the more remarkable given the increased prevalence of pathological behaviors relating to the accumulation of money and commodities in our society. And yet, as this book shows, recent developments in psychoanalysis offer the tools for a more sophisticated and less reductionistic analysis of disorders relating to acquisition and hoarding; while, in turn, shedding valuable light on the critical issue of compulsive and addictive behavior patterns.

Any study of the role of acquisitiveness in pathology cannot dispense with references to the influence which cultural factors play in nourishing such behaviors in our society (there is an important distinction being drawn here between "nourishing" and "causing"). As Jules Henry stated "psychopathology is the final outcome of all that is wrong with a culture."[2] Such an approach is consonant with the more inclusive models of social work practice.[3] However, the relationship of individual pathology and social influencing factors is not simply linear causal. Rather, as Philip Rieff explains the connection, "history changes the expression of neurosis even if it does not change the underlying mechanisms."[4] Clement (1982) and Richards warn against the dangers of overextending psychiatric models (such as narcissism) for broad social analysis and cultural critique. Christopher Lasch, himself the target of much of this criticism of the use of psychoanalytic categories for macroanalysis, has warned against the "confusion" it can create.[5]

However, each society appears to have its own "prevailing forms of suffering".[6] It is one matter to argue that social factors help to nourish the development of a particular form of pathology, and another matter entirely to see one form of societal structure as the cause of that pathology. In an article on "Narcissism and the Crisis of Capitalism", Russell Jacoby, following Otto Kernberg's assertion that narcissistic patients are "often not dysfunctional but well adjusted," draws the broad conclusion that such a "character disorder is, therefore, not an individual, but a social disorder."[7] There is a sense in which such a statement might be considered helpful. The very definition, for example, of what is seen in any society as a disorder of excess is interwoven with cultural norms. Witness the extreme misuse of such norms in the concept of 'adraptomania', which was once used to pathologize slaves who repeatedly tried to escape the plantation.[8] As one theorist of addiction states "excess is not absolute but is personally and socially defined."[9] Also, the very reticence to discuss issues of money noted above is itself a cultural factor which must be accounted for. As Wilhelm Reich was perhaps the first to note, "every social order creates those character forms which it needs for its preservation."[10] This book will argue that what Reich said about the effects of social structure on character applies with even greater force in the case of the consumer pathologies.[11] Money is an over-determined symbol in our society, and there are many ways in which it enters into pathological behaviors. This chapter will be concerned with only one of these behaviors, albeit a very prevalent and devastating one, namely, the compulsive acquisition and hoarding of commodities.

Borrowing from Alasdair MacIntyre's highly influential work, *After Virtue* the descriptive term *pleonexia* will be used as a convenient label for this disorder. Although coming from the Greeks, the term is part of the English language, being defined there as avarice or covetousness.[12] But as Webster (1986) points out the Greek original is literally "to have or want more." MacIntyre, therefore, finds Friedrich Nietzsche's *"haben und mehrwollhaben"* (iterally, to have and to want to possess more) as a particularly felicitous translation. The standard Greek-English Lexicon refers to Plato's and Aristotle's use as 'excess gain,' "a larger share of a thing."[13] The important point for MacIntyre is that translations, such as J.S. Mill's, in terms of the vice of avarice miss the point that the problem is with "acquisitiveness as such," a characteristic behavior that in our consumer culture is not recognized "to be a vice at all."[14] In a more recent study, MacIntyre draws a distinction which will be important for this book.[15] He takes issue with Hobbes' translation of the term by the desire word 'greed.' MacIntyre notes that pleonexia is actually "a disposition," something very different from "one motive for activities of acquisition." It is important to see pleonexia as "the name of the tendency to engage in such activities simply for their own sake."[16] The distinction that MacIntyre is drawing here is one central to understanding Freud's motivatioinal theory and his use of such terms as "unconscious desire" and "intention" (subtle differences in the use of desire, want and intention will be ignored for purposes of the analysis in this section; see chapter 3 below for more on these terms). It is, therefore, of prime importance to any project which hopes to shed light on the nature of addiction through the use of psychoanalytic categories (for this reason these issues will come up again in relevant sections of subsequent chapters). The important distinction that MacIntyre is drawing here is one which he elaborated on earlier in his work on *The Unconscious*, and that can be traced to Gilbert Ryle.[17] For Ryle a disposition is an ability, tendency, or proneness to act or react, or fail to act or react, in a certain way under certain circumstances.

In other words, a disposition is a behavior pattern or quality of character. Those individuals who have the "character trait" of acquisitiveness demonstrate a tendency to aggrandizement no matter what their motives or intentions. For humans, dispositions always include the possibility of avowal of intention, even if, in the case of the neurotic, it may require psychoanalysis to bring unconscious motives to consciousness.[18]

Under most circumstances we can determine what a person desires or intends either by asking her or by observing her behavior. Under normal circumstances, we do not question the authority of an individual about what he or she wants.[19] Behaviorists, influenced by Gilbert Ryle, wished to restrict the use of such terms to observable actions. For Ryle, as just noted, a disposition is a certain inclination toward a specific action.[20] However, Freud was most interested in those problematic cases where what a person maintains and her actions are at variance. Freud's great contribution was to extend the use of the concept 'motive' to make it applicable to involuntary behavior. This extension, as Thomas Smythe maintains, is all the more important and understandable in the case of compulsive behaviors, where unconscious motives play an even greater role.[21] It is in such compulsive actions that there is often a conflict between avowed desires and those denied; the use of unconscious desires is, at least in part, to explain the strength and persistence of actions which the agent often disavows. The dispositional analysis of motives, in this expanded version, postulates the existence of unconscious *tendencies* which constitute systems of wants rather than a want in isolation.[22] It is this systems aspect of our wants and corresponding beliefs which helps to explain their overdetermined role in compulsive behaviors. It also helps to explain how social factors can influence such behaviors: for as Alston maintains a want" makes action tendencies susceptible to increase by beliefs; in other words, it brings it about that our beliefs have an effect on what we do."[23] And he adds, such influences can be subject to repression just as desires can.[24]

The distinction which MacIntyre makes between an individual motive, such as greed, and a disposition, such as pleonexia, is the difference between a particular aroused desire and a more latent behavior pattern or quality of character. Those individuals who have the character trait of acquisitiveness demonstrate a tendency to aggrandizement no matter what their particular motives or intentions.[25] Whereas greed has been an almost universal motive, it is this latter tendency which MacIntyre sees as a defining characteristic of modern society.

The important point is that our social norms, unlike those of Greece and most previous societies, judge the tendency to acquisitiveness *simpliciter* as unproblematic.[26] However, Bernard Williams provides an important modification to this use of classical philosophy, in his masterful, *Sources of the Self: the Making of Modern Identity*.[27] He demonstrates how the positive transformation from classical morality, with its aristocratic bias, to our "affirmation of everyday life," contributed to our egalitarian ethos. With this important caveat in mind, it is important to reiterate that the use of pleonexia, in this study, is only for the illumination it gives to consumer pathology, and not as moral or political critique.

Ryan Balot, in his seminal work on the concept of pleonexia, makes a qualification of MacIntyre's interpretation that is of great importance to this study of consumer pathology. Balot argues that pleonexia refers, not to acquisitiveness as such, but to "an *excessive* desire to get more."[28] It is this insatiable and driven aspect of material desire that is its true problematic feature. This feature is captured in a saying of Epicurus: "Nothing is enough for the man to whom enough is too little."And it is this new, excessive, propensity to consume that is nourished by an economic system based on limitless growth. The philosopher, Amélie Rorty notes one way that this happens: "market-based, consumer-oriented economic systems generate invidious comparisons as a way of increasing consumption."[29] It is important to distinguish here between the motive of greed, which has always been with us, and this new tendency of pleonexia. Historian Stanton Coblentz shows the uniqueness of our time, where from infancy we are "thoroughly taught that life's flower and summit is acquisition."[30] As Erich Fromm put it "man has transformed himself into a "homo consumens," a new "character type" with an "insatiable" appetite for commodities.[31] This new character is narcissitically "consumed in its consuming".[32] What are the major differences which distinguish this frenzy of acquisition from consumption patterns in other cultures?

Social anthropologists who have examined the role of goods in traditional societies point to several key differences from our modern pattern.[33] Douglas and Isherwood point to the "rituals of reciprocity" in which goods make and maintain social relationships. A good example is the Kula trade examined by Malinowski, where an emphasis on *accumulation* would have destroyed the basic function of the exchange system, namely the social relationship between the exchanges themselves.[34]The importance of this example for hoarding should be obvious.

On the other hand, "large-scale consumption patterns" are seen only where goods are used as "weapons of exclusion"; for example, in societies like the Yurok (and like our own) in which "unfettered individualism" characterizes the social structure. Art, culture, and solidarity rituals are at a minimum in such societies.[35] Such groups have often been forced into traditional patterns. Stanton Coblentz notes that, even in these exceptional societies, they show a pride in ownership and display. Paradoxically, this arises from a rejection of possessiveness, where the display and enhancement of the person's ego comes from demonstrating they do not need these objects of value.[36] The similarities with our own "throw-away" society, as well as with Veblen's 1925 analysis of its "leisure class" rituals are striking. In such individualistic societies goods take on a new and aggressive meaning.

This alienation from traditional symbols and structures stemming from the "commoditization process" was documented by

Michael Taussig in his influential study of two South American societies.[37] Taussig contrasts Marcel Mauss' classic study of *The Gift* rituals of the Maori with Marx's famous concept of commodity fetishism to show the major change in the social function of goods from pre-capitalist to capitalist societies. For the Maori, as well as Taussig's South Americans, goods only have meaning as personalized signs for social relationships. What is different about commodity fetishism is the effect these exchanges have on transforming social relationships into relationships between commodities.[38] Taussig shows how traditional societies attempt to resist this change by incorporating it within their mythic structure of evil and the devil. Jean Baudrillard argues that a large part of our societies difficulties with "*consommation*" stem from the lack of a similar myth to explain this reification of commodities and relations.[39]

The historical process by which this change in the meaning and function of commodities has come about in our western society, and its psychological effects is the topic of an ambitious and stimulating analysis by Colin Campbell.[40] The anthropologists have shown that commodities have a dual function: they serve both to satisfy needs and to communicate meaning as part of a hermeneutic order or signifying system. They have applied this anthropological analysis directly to our culture as "privileged discourse through and about objects".[41] Campbell has documented a modern form of hedonism, with its roots ironically in our puritan past, one which employs a strong role for imagination, as the central change leading to our consumer-oriented society. Campbell argues that it was in the eighteenth century rather than the nineteenth that this new form of hedonism began to flourish. He demonstrated the shortcomings of three popular models of the rise of consumer culture: (first) "instinctivism," which postulates an "acquisitive instinct".[42] This is the view that our wants and desires are biological in origin and therefore can be assimilated to the category of *needs*.[43] There are many problems with this effort to equate wants and needs: (1) it was historically used to try to discount the influence of social and cultural factors; (2) it traditionally has functioned in economic theory as something just presumed, which limits empirical investigation; (3) by equating humans with lower animals, like "jackdaws" with their innate disposition to acquire shiny objects, it ignores the "extreme plasticity" of our acquisitive behavior and makes it very difficult to explain, what Campbell argues is a similar predisposition toward getting rid of goods (one lacking in those with hoarding disorder); (4) it suffers from the fallacy of begging the question by assuming what it claims to prove by invoking the desire for a commodity as evidence that we have a "latent want" for commodities.[44] Campbell argues against the view (most closely associated with Abraham Maslow) of a needs/wants hierarchy — the theory that wants are higher-order motives added to a base of biological needs in an ascending order of increased civilization. Not only is the anthropological evidence against such a view, it also has overtones of "evolutionary ethnocentrism", a view which associates a person's higher ends with the ideology of western civilization. But most importantly for my purposes here, this hierarchical view suffers from the many problems associated with any motivational theory based on biological needs. Campbell cites only the tautological flavor given by the tendency to "explain" the *satisfaction* of a need at one level by postulating the appearance of a 'higher' need.[45]

It is important to point out, however, that the ability to distinguish between ones "true needs" and artificial needs imposed by ideology is an essential part of healthy human development.[46] The role that determining ones true needs plays in a healthy sense of personal identity has been repeatedly demonstrated by experts on hoarding disorder.[47] However, as William James famously pointed out, the exact line between what a person calls me and mine is not an easy one to draw.[48] It is a principle argument of this book that culture plays a key role in where the line is drawn, and that this is central to understanding all the forms of consumer disorder.

The second group of models criticized by Campbell is the various

forms of "manipulationism". This is the view which attributes

consumer demand to a conspiracy created by advertisers and

businessmen.[49] This model, in sharp contrast to instinctivism, might be

characterized as the nurture view; one which recognizes only

acquired tendencies, attributing a passive role to the consumer.

Campbell notes a continuum of manipulationists, from the extreme

idea that mere exposure to advertisements creates desires to the trivial

views which hold that the media simply influences demand.

However, he is concerned with those who maintain that consumers

are consciously 'forced' to act against their own inclinations, and

often against their own self interest. Campbell offers the following

arguments against this model: (1) advertising is only one of the

many cultural influences acting on the consumer (he doesn't

mention the most obvious counterforce, the so-called consumer-

protection agencies); (2) the great heterogeniety of marketable goods

and audiences modifying the effects of media messages; (3) the large

body of empirical evidence which shows that consumers do not simply

ingest commercial messages in an unthinking manner. Rather such

messages interact with existing dispositions in a much more complex

and active manner. The whole existence of market research, after all,

is predicated on the need to discover what the pre-existing dreams, desires and wishes of the consumer are and to design ads which appeal to them. Campbell argues that it cannot be the underlying motivational structure of consumers which is being manipulated, since it is this very structure of dispositions which is being accounted for in such research. Campbell draws a distinction here between the exploitation of existing motives and manipulation which creates new motives. He further distinguishes between the manipulation of the symbolic meanings attached to various products and the manipulation of the underlying motives which may become associated with such symbols. In short, what advertisers do is manipulate messages rather than individuals. This argument changes the focus to the issue of how do symbolic structures influence the creation of new wants and desires (the limitations of this symbolic turn in the argument will be examined in the discussion of Baudrillard later in this chapter). Campbell argues that it was utilitarianism which artificially designated the "intrinsic utility" of the product as the sole source of gratification rather than any images or ideas which might be associated with that product. Words, images, and symbolic meanings, Campbell maintains play a very "real" role in gratification.[50]

The economic utilitarians wanted to maintain that the market was based on rational calculation of motives; therefore, any introduction of emotion and imagination would indicate manipulation of the consumer. However, as Campbell clearly shows, the role of affective attachment is as basic to consumption, if not more so, than rational calculation; so that the mere existence of an emotional component to advertising does not signal manipulation. In sum, this model ignores the differences between manipulation and exploitation, and reduces the consumer to a purely passive receptor of artificial wants.[51]

The last of Galbraith's three models of consumer demand which Campbell criticizes he calls "the Veblenesque Perspective".[52] Thorsten Veblen was highly critical of what he saw to be the inadequate psychology which served as the foundation of economic theory in his day.[53] Veblen's highly influential view *sees* the consumer as motivated primarily by status emulation and such motives as envy and pride.[54] Keynes called such effects "needs of the second class", i.e. the "insatiable need" to "keep abreast or ahead" of others.[55] Veblen was interested in "the surplus of motives which economic abundance made possible and inevitable", and in the "seductive" quality of these motives.[56] He introduced a non-rational component to consumer demand; and one which he maintained could not be reduced simply to hedonism. He also saw that "the same objects may be pursued for a variety of motives, and a variety of objects for the same motive."[57]. Veblen's model has the decided advantage of seeing the consumer as an active participant in the creation of wants.

Campbell argues, however, that Veblen's account, though an important step toward recognizing the importance of cultural and symbolic factors in consumer demand, operates from too simplistic a theory of motivation. For one thing, Veblen concentrates on the symbol of price, but there are many other messages which the consumer may wish to convey by the purchase of a product, for example, taste and style. Similarly, the "other-directed" influences motivating the consumer are more complex than Veblen recognized, in that there are often a variety of different categories of individuals with which the consumer may relate in "positive, negative, comparative, and normative" ways.[58] What is more, Campbell argues, Veblen assumes an "aggressive" theory of motivation, one which sees the individual as motivated by "a race" to "outdo" others in conspicuous consumption, rather than the more "defensive" stance of maintaining one's position in line.[59] Again, Campbell maintains that studies in reference group theory demonstrate a more complex system of influences. Veblen's own model is complicated by his stratification theory which postulates a leisure class at the top which sets an ideal standard (both moral and aesthetic) which becomes the source of emulation by the rest of the community. Campbell offers two

116

criticisms of this view: first, that Veblen confuses competition with imitation. Rivalry between an intimate group of competitors, such as "athletes," is not the same as social mobility based on adopting a new lifestyle. Furthermore, as Campbell argues, "innovation" can be just as important as "imitation" for economic success. Also, in our fast paced consumer culture, there is often a conflict about the very definition of what determines social status. [60] Secondly, Campbell argues that Veblen assumes a homogeneity of values which simply doesn't exist in our highly mobile society, where the richest classes do not dictate fashion (as will be seen below, Georg Simmel offered a more sophisticated analysis of the social role of fashion and envy).

But Campbell's most important criticism of Veblen, from the viewpoint of this book, concerns the limitations of his psychological assumptions. For Veblen, the primary lesson to be learned about modern consumer behavior is what it tells us about social status. But, as Campbell notes, there is another significant aspect of such behavior; namely, what it can tell us about the nature of individual character. Individual subjective states, such as a motive to enhance self-esteem, are used to "explain" the insatiability of consumption, but this is no more explanatory than to ascribe this behavior to a motive of "greed." Campbell has expanded on these important distinctions in his more recent work. He draws some important distinctions between conscious and unconscious motives and intentions; and, offers a more useful definition of a *motive* as "a subjectively meaningful experience, composed of thoughts and emotions, which prompts an individual to act."[61]

Finally, Campbell holds that Veblen's famous thesis fails to distinguish the uniquely modern and western characteristics of consumer behavior — namely, its insatiability and never-ending desire for novelty.[62] However, when Campbell comes to describe his own model, he disappoints for very similar reasons, by assuming a too "rationalized" and autonomous hedonism to fit the uniquely modern picture of consumer reality.

Campbell's model of "modern autonomous imaginative hedonism" does point to the air of unreality which seems to pervade out consumer culture, which he calls its "as-if" quality. The day-dreaming, self-illusory quality of consumer behavior is captured in such fictional characters as Walter Mitty and Billy Liar. The day-dreams of consumers are attached to the acquisition of objects, but are unfulfilled once these objects have been possessed, leaving a need for further fantasy acquisitions.[63] Campbell sets himself the formidable task of explaining this complex behavior through a number of historical paradoxes: how a culture of pleasure-seeking could take root in puritan soil; how it could receive its energy from a Romantic ethic which spent much of its time condemning the "waste of getting and spending"; how a disposition to acquire could combine such seemingly contradictory features as the primacy of the fantasies associated with the object over possessing it, the pleasure in longing with the disillusionment with gratification, the never-ending, restless quality of acquiring with just as rapid a disposal of objects. The latter, of course, is missing in hoarding behavior. It is no wonder that his analysis falls short of explaining this daunting agenda, not to speak of the lack of desire to discard in hoarding (something he did not attempt to address). However, Campbell does have some interesting psychological insights about the role of the ideal self and the search for perfection in narcissism, which will prove useful in the concluding chapter of this book.

In an effort to combat the simplistic model of the manipulationist and to demonstrate the role of the individual consumer's autonomy and "rationalized" hedonism, Campbell underestimates the social pressures, as well as the impulsive-forces which nourish the addiction to consume. As one author summed it up forcefully, "compulsive spending is our most communicable disease."[64] This more pessimistic side of our peculiar form of hedonism has been the subject of many social critics.[65] Christopher Lasch, another noted critic of this darker side of consumption, has objected entirely to the use of the term "hedonism" in connection with consumerism, because it covers up the role played by acquisitiveness in our "uneasiness and chronic anxiety".[66]

The futurist critic William Simon (building on the insights of Emile Durkheim and Robert Merton) has labeled this aspect of consumerism "the anomie of affluence".[67] Simon points to the increasing lack of gratification (both "consummatory" and "constraining") in consumer behavior, and how this tends to loosen community bonds. The very imaginative form of pleasure-seeking, which Campbell argues convincingly distinguishes modern consumer society, encourages this atomization and impulsiveness. There is a substitution of individual for social metaphors, with a corresponding shift in advertising from products that symbolize high social status to personal experiences that show your unique superior attributes or personal qualities.[68]

Simon refers to the great early French sociologist and social critic Emile Durkheim's influential concept of anomie. Durkheim understood, as this book has argued, that any explanation of complex human behavior, such as consumer pathology, requires a full appreciation of the role of internalized social norms and values. His pioneering work on suicide showed a paradoxical correlation between increased luxury and unhappiness. Influenced by ideas from

Schopenhauer and others about the eternally insatiable nature of desire, Durkheim argued that individual's needed the restraint or "modulation" of appetites provided by internalized social norms. He added that what was a luxury to earlier generations had been transformed into needs. He asserted that it was these unregulated, insatiable desires that had led to unhappiness amidst plenty. [69] Simon's own analysis of this disposition to consume underscores the same role for fantasy and imagination which Campbell calls attention to. Simon points to the "psychologically overdetermined" quality of this dynamic. Comparing Durkheim and Freud, Simon notes that even painful emotions, such as those related to feelings of deprivation, "often amplify fantasy far beyond those that reality can meet."[70] It is this overdetermined quality which plays a psychological role in the insatiability and addictive aspect of pleonexia. Simon offers a typology of those characters who adaptively respond to these social forces, with the pleonexic seeming to combine features of types three and four: type three, "the compulsive achiever", is the individual who seems compelled to achieve compulsively because she is someone who does not know how to find compatible ways of finding satisfaction or fulfillment.[71] This person focuses on the rewards of "having made it", but is driven by "an unquenchable thirst" to achieve more and more. The fourth type, the "conforming deviant" searches endlessly for new pleasures, new ways of achieving satisfaction. But, this pursuit of novel experiences is also inexhaustible and all-consuming.[72] However, Simon leans too heavily in the direction of Durkheim and away from Freud in his concept of "sociomorphic thinking".[73] It is not a question of imputing aspects of social life to the organism. Rather, an interactionist model is closer to the facts, as can be seen in Stuart Ewen's most recent contribution, *All Consuming Images*.[74]

Ewen, like Campbell and Simon, gives a large role to what he calls "the capitalization of imagination" in the "rise of the commodity self".[75] However, Ewen's analysis has the added virtue that it acknowledges both the "liberating" and "oppressive" aspects of the new commercial order. In an earlier work, Ewen exposed the claims of the pioneers of marketing that they were simply extending democracy as rhetoric masking a strong authoritarian and conformist motivation.[76] In *All Consuming Images,* Ewen presents the case for this *freedom* as a "fragmentation and deception"; and *style* as the dreamlike release of unconscious id impulses. Campbell could argue, with some justification, that Ewen is simply another in a long line of manipulationists. However, it is Ewen's emphasis on the conflicting outcomes of liberation for the self, "both disorienting and promising", which helps to explain the dynamism that Campbell wished to understand. Ewen demonstrates how the advertising

122

industry takes advantage of the ego's dream to achieve wholeness and identity by transforming the objects of desire (commodities) into subjective images. But Ewen does not ignore the part played by the consumer in this tension between inner self and outer image (reminiscent of Nietzsche's famous quote at the opening of this chapter). Ewen argues that two forces led to this emphasis on the realization of personal identity through style: (1) a new concept of freedom (articulated by Jean-Paul Sartre) which is predicated on personal self-determined action; and (2) the routinization and fragmentation of production which denied the actualization of wholeness and identity in the workplace. This left only the consumer arena as the place for "the desire for freedom, the freedom to desire". In the twisted logic of the marketplace, "To have is to do".[77]

It was Georg Simmel who was arguably the first and most sophisticated analyst of this fragmenting of the self in consumer society. In two works in particular, *The Philosophy of Money* and his essay "Fashion", Simmel pointed to the role that commodities came to play in filling the void left by the growing fragmentation and individuality of modern (especially urban) life.[78] It was, Simmel argues, this psychological drive of the ego to achieve wholeness and identity that made acquisitiveness more obsessive in nature. Like

Marx, Simmel was concerned with the alienation of relationships brought about by their growing commodification and exchange nature. But unlike Marx, Simmel's concern was mostly with the effects of such alienation on our inner life (*unsres Inneren*), the domination of the objective over the subjective, "the dissolution of fixed contents in the fluid elements of the soul". Also unlike Marx, Simmel was mostly concerned with the effects of consumer commodities, and with the "*neuasthenie*," the nervous tension created by the restless and insatiable quality of consumer pursuits.[79]

Simmel was one of the first and most astute theorists to analyze some of the important features of "the remarkable psychological mania for accumulation".[80] The first of these features Simmel examined under the headings "cynicism" and "the blasé attitude".[81] Simmel argued that these are defensive responses to the rapidly shifting stimuli of consumer society and urban life.[82] It is significant that, in *The Philosophy of Money,* Simmel contrasts cynicism and the blasé attitude with greed and avarice, two of the most common misleading translations of pleonexia; and, that, in the original German, Simmel writes of the *Zynischer Disposition.* What Simmel means by Zynismus is a tendency to level all values, which, he maintains, is nourished by money's capacity to reduce values to one common denominator.[83] Unlike the gambler, who attempts to find meaning in the meaninglessness of coincidence, the cynic is concerned with the "disparagement of all old values." This "subjective reflex" has another related effect in the blasé attitude, the effect of "satiated enjoyment," "*erschöpfende Genüsse,* literally drained or exhausted enjoyment (*erschopft* also means "to spend"). Simmel composes two basic character types (both of whom, he argues, are more similar than is usually recognized, and, therefore, often combined in the same individual): the person who gets pleasure out of wasting or spending and the miser.[84] Simmel maintains that the pleasure involved in wasting needs to be contrasted with the pleasure in ostentation and in acquisition or consumption. The former is fleeting, and like the abstract and leveling quality of money, it is independent of the use-value of the object purchased.

Simmel anticipated recent clinical findings about the irrational aspects of compulsive spending and acquiring. He notes that "the attractions of the instant overshadow the rational evaluation of either money or commodities." He adds that any enjoyment involved does not reside in the objects purchased, but rather in the process; and, that the insatiable nature of this behavior means that the pleonexic is "doomed never to find repose and permanency; the moment of his possession of an object coincides with the negation of his enjoyment (p.250)." Simmel's model combines a strongly biological view of the effects of excessive nervous excitation with a social psychology of urban capitalism. On the biological side is the belief that the rapid and frequent bombardment of the senses creates a "hyperaesthesia" (sensitivity to touch), and a corresponding defensive reaction of indifference — the nerves simply cease to react after too much stimulation. On the psychological side, this same restless and fragmented social life helps to create an equally fragmented and fluid sense of self which leaves the individual prey to the obsessive quality of fashion. The addict attempts to incorporate commodities into the self but by their very nature they remain separate thereby leading to frustration.[85] On the social side, the abstract nature of money takes away the kind of controls that would come from the "consummatory enjoyment of the object"; leading to an immoderate and irrational pursuit without external or internal constraints. This virtual or abstract aspect of capitalism, of course, has increased tremendously since he wrote. Simmel recognized that these addictive tendencies would only be multiplied by the growth of a credit society, though he could not imagine the extent to which this has become the case.[86]

Finally, Simmel extended the Marxian concept of the fetishism of commodities by analyzing the psychological effect when commodities become increasingly external and autonomous to the consumer. External and material values take on a greater

126

importance, with a corresponding devaluation of the inner self; a process encouraged by the fashion industry. This impoverishment of the internal reinforces the obsessive quality of buying in a vicious circle of a pathological nature. The consumer becomes oppressed by the products of his own labor. There is restricted room in such a society, for the self to express its will and feelings, adding to the growing tendency to "covetousness and addiction."[87] The abstraction or alienation is even more pronounced when it comes to money, as "the significance of money replaces the significance of things."[88] This abstraction process has become even more pronounced since Simmel's time.[89] The abstract quality of Marx's exchange value analyzed by Simmel is extended and nicely complicated (i.e. opened up) still further by the analysis of the French social critic Jean Baudrillard (without mention, however, of Simmel's pioneering work). Baudrillard draws heavily from the linguists and anthropologists of the structuralist school for his critical tools, but also increasingly from psychoanalysis. The anthropologists (including non-structuralists like Mary Douglas) demonstrated how the commodity combines its natural use function with its role as a source of ritualized meaning for a society (e.g. the gift function). Baudrillard, in his early work starts from the assumption that commodities function as a system of meaning, like a language or a kinship system, and proceeds to analyze the psychosocial implications of this fact for modern western societies.[90] In addition to satisfying needs the commodity also serves to communicate meanings in social relations. However, in a later work Baudrillard greatly complicates his earlier analysis, coming up with four logically distinct (but never experientially separate) categories of significance for commodities: (1) the functional or use value; (2) an economic exchange value (Marx's exchange value); (3) a symbolic exchange (*l'échange symbolique* - *e.g.* the gift which symbolizes the social relationships of giver and receiver, like a wedding ring); and, most abstract of all (4) a logic of sign value.[91] Interestingly, Baudrillard's move to increasing abstraction, from the symbol function (with its alleged grounding in desire) to the sign, parallels a similar move in the psychoanalytic analysis of the psychological role of commodities.[92]

In his earlier works, Baudrillard starts from a critique of the rationalist and utilitarian concept of homo economicus (in its modern form of homo psychoeconomicus), the view which holds simply that commodities function to satisfy natural needs.[93] In a more recent work, he expands this criticism to include Marx's theory that human need invests commodities with value.[94] Ironically, according to Baudrillard, Marx ends up contributing to the ideology of modern capitalism by failing to see that it is the other way around; i.e. it is the commodity system and use value which produce this ideology of desire as their rationalization. Baudrillard points to the basically empty and tautological character of this utilitarian myth. The individual consumes a particular commodity because she wishes to conform to a certain social group, and the individual belongs to the group because she consumes this particular commodity. This "naive psychology" of the consumer as motivated by biologically given needs and "confronted by real objects as sources of satisfaction" hides an "unconscious social logic" in the same way in which the manifest dream content masks over unconscious material.[95] Baudrillard accepts the advantages of the manipulationist's view which holds that it is the need to generate demand brought about by almost unlimited productivity, rather than this classical notion of a demand driven by individual need or desire, which is the dynamic of consumer society. This manipulationist concept of the "conditioning of needs" through advertising and marketing techniques is the way in which *"freedom of choice is imposed on [the consumer].*"[96] Baudrillard's critique of this manipulationist social theory (which includes Marx's famous concept of alienation) is his major contribution to the analysis of this book. The manipulationists (Galbraith is his principle example) accept a false theory of motivation based on a notion of fundamentally stable human needs and drives which place a limit on consumer impulses unless they are manipulated by "artificial accelerators."[97]

Baudrillard takes strong issue with the whole notion of "artificial" needs (a notion which goes back to Marx, 1973). He points out that, since from the perspective of the consumer the gratification is experienced as equally "real" in each product, there is no basis for defining what is artificial from what is not.[98] Furthermore, the motivational theory of the manipulationists suffers from a simplification of a more complicated psychological process, with its idea that one need is produced for each new object created, thus making "the basic psyche of the consumer into a shop window or display."[99] Baudrillard criticizes the manipulationist's theory as too atomistic. He takes issue with any hedonistic version of this naturalistic reductionism, pointing out that in modern society consumption has become a citizen's *duty*.[100] He argues that in our society use value has become a rationalization, a simulacrum for the social role of the commodity. It is *"as elements of a system"* and not simply as the *"relation between an individual and an object"* that needs and pleasures are to be understood.[101] Baudrillard would also take issue with Colin Campbell's history of the emergence of a modern hedonism out of the ashes of our puritan past. There has been no such "revolution of morals", the puritan ethos is still a major force in consumer society; in fact it is what gives consumption and need "its compulsive and unlimited character."[102] Baudrillard can maintain this paradoxical view because, at this stage in his analysis, he sees the forces which motivate consumption as simply the extension of productive forces which work by defining subjects as needing objects (an extension, of course, of Weber and Marx). Baudrillard attempts to move the commodity to a more "fluid and unconscious field of signification", a more abstract level for the social forces of desire.[103] At such a level, the objects of desire are"substitutable like the symptoms of hysterical or psychosomatic conversion." To trace a need to a specific object is like performing traditional therapy on a specific hysterical symptom, rather than treating the *"general hysteria"* (emphasis in original).The specific symptom is merely the expression of something insatiable because it is founded on a want or lack.[104] It is this general craving for social meaning, rather than a specific object or pleasure that is the driving force behind insatiable consumer behavior. Unlike pleasure, which is something autonomous and final, consumption, for Baudrillard is a collective endeavor, an obligation for the individual, governed by a social code of interchangeable signs.[105]

The object (T.V., car, washing machine) takes on the unconscious role as "a token of recognition, of integration, of social legitimacy."[106] The compulsion to consume is not psychologically determined, in the sense of a biological drive or instinct; nor is it simply a matter of the compulsion of fashion.[107] Rather it is because of its idealistic quality, and the fact that consumption of objects takes the place of interpersonal relations that it is "irresponsible."[108] This view goes beyond the psychoanalytical view of advertising which sees it as unleashing id forces (*"forces profondes"*) which elude the control of the superego.[109] Like Simmel, Baudrillard is aware of the new dimension in the compulsion to spend brought about by the introduction of credit.[110] The abstract or idealized quality of the sign is even more pronounced in a credit economy. In such an economy, a given commodity is even freed from its specific psychological meaning, from its specific use, and from its commercial role as product, and, instead, assumes the value of fashion, i.e., the atomization of social relations.[111]

In his earliest work, Baudrillard borrows heavily from the French psychoanalysts in his examination of the unconscious fantasies and defenses generated by commodities and fashion.[112] However, beginning with *L'échange symbolique et la Mort* (1976) Baudrillard's views on psychoanalysis become increasingly critical, as well as abstract.[113]

Baudrillard's works are, for the most part, completely devoid of empirical references. His social theory is highly abstract, lacking in concrete historical materiality, in any grounding in non-mental and nonlinguistic reality. Many of his later works, especially, have a strongly nihilistic message and revolve around concepts like illusion (*leuvre)*, simulacre and the imaginary. In the words of one critic, his work "recognizes nothing beyond a play of mirrors destined endlessly to reflect signs and images that have no meaning outside the infinite regress of definitions of definitions."[114]

For the purpose of advancing understanding of the social forces effecting the development of pleonexia, the work of William Leiss on satisfaction, needs and commodities is of greater importance than any of the previous authors examined, including Baudrillard.[115] Leiss concentrates his concern on the negative psychological effects of our high consumption life-style. More specifically he focuses on the instability of personality, as well as certain pathological internal "dispositions" engendered by the bewildering array of rapidly changing commodities.

Every individual, in no matter what culture, must find a way to match her needs to the opportunities available for satisfaction, Leiss maintains.[116] What I have called pleonexia, and Leiss calls a "high-consumption life-style" paradoxically leads to a lack of concern about "specific wants," while simultaneously occupying a greater proportion of the individual's overall "time and resources."[117] The crucial result of this process is a splintering of cohesive need "into progressively smaller component parts."This, in turn, leads to a corresponding breakdown of the individual's "coherent personality structure."[118]Leiss is correct to argue that every individual has an essential need to develop personal identity, self-esteem and the esteem of others. As a result of this human need, certain "internal dispositions or personality traits" are cultivated, as well as a corresponding concern for external appearances. However, as a result of the constant introduction of, rapidly changing commodities there is a "fragmentation" of personal identity. The great quantity and variety of material objects produced by our "high-intensity market" encourages this breaking down of personal identity, followed by the "delicate art" of reintegrating identity as a consumer personality, conforming to the image and values promoted by marketers. The result is that an increasing amount of time is spent acquiring ever more commodities.[119]

What Leiss has in mind can best be seen in the case of personal appearance. The vast number of products for the adornment and enhancement of the body, which must be combined in the proper arrangements and proportions to be socially acceptable, provides the consumer with a confusing and constantly changing array of choices for personal expression (and can easily become the vector point for self-esteem problems). This contrasts sharply with more traditional societies, Leiss would argue, where personal expression can take more predictable and stable forms.

Some of the most important observations which Leiss makes concern the ancient issue of the instability of wants. Leiss argues that, at least in high-consumption societies, the link "between desires and types of satisfaction" is a lot more complex and ambiguous than is usually assumed.[120] He sees a breakdown in what he calls "craft knowledge," the degree of familiarity with objects, which in traditional societies helps the individual interpret his/her environment in order to make a proper assessment of the suitability of commodities to meet needs. Leiss uses the example of environmental cues and obesity. However, he never mentions Stanley Schachter's ingenious experiments, which showed that obese subjects are affected by external cues such as the sight of food, its availability, and apparent passage of time, whereas subjects of normal weight respond more directly to inner sensations. Yet, this appears to be the sort of evidence that Leiss is relying on here. Schachter's work shows, once again, the importance of symbolic factors, such as "labeling", in consumption.[121] The obese person, Leiss argues, misinterprets the relationship between her needs and available means for satisfying them, thereby leading to damaging over consumption. Leiss cites evidence that obesity, in some individuals at least, is related to anxiety and depression, which in turn is related to such social needs as "for acceptance, approval, and achievement". The psychosocial cause of obesity, on this view, comes from a preoccupation with satisfying ones need for food, with a corresponding fixation on the environmental "messages, cues, and stimuli" associated with gratifying this need. This narrowing of wants to one type of commodity, for Leiss, is contrary to the "normal pattern" of spreading ones "wants among different sets of commodities." [122]

Leiss fails to show how the individual becomes fixated on this particular mode of gratification, and the link between social needs for acceptance, etc., and overconsumption is not entirely clear; but Leiss is, nonetheless, pointing to how the high-consumption society encourages individuals to "depend upon social cues to guide them in deciding how extensively to use any commodity or sets of commodities" to gratify their internal needs. Pleonexia, Leiss would maintain, "results from refracting all interpersonal and market stimuli through a particular fixation" on a commodity or set of commodities. [123]

What is more, the effect of social pressures is to encourage the individual "to shift his ensemble of satisfactions and dissatisfactions continually from a smaller to a larger set of commodities (or sets of commodities with more elaborate characteristics"). [124] The reason for this enlargement in purchases is

136

the "destabilization" and "fragmentation" of needs into smaller and smaller units described earlier. What Leiss is describing is a failure in that socialization process which would have normally assisted the individual to develop a "holistic" and integrated personality for interpreting her needs (as will be seen in the next chapter, the concept of 'integration' is a key one in psychoanalytic analysis of character). The high-consumption society, in part at least, has this effect because it deflects other avenues of self-fulfillment into an exclusive satisfaction through the use of commodities.

Note that Leiss is not arguing for a simple manipulationist view, one in which society or powerful groups within a society work to create a new set of artificial needs. Reciprocal needs for such things as approval and affirmation exist in every society. Leiss notes that there is nothing unique about the coupling of specific emotional states with culturally defined wants and needs. What is unique to our consumer society is that "the linkages between desires and types of satisfactions are highly ambiguous."[125]

However, it would be inappropriate to attribute the fragmentation process, as Leiss tends to do, solely to economic factors; without taking into account such other factors as the breakdown in shared rituals which give integrity and coherence to personal identity (partly through the use of symbolically understood roles).

Nonetheless, Leiss is pointing to the important fact that commodities as "materially-symbolic entities" incorporate the "dualistic character of human needing", that is, its inseparable material and social characteristics.[126] The tendency of our consumer society to lead to compulsive behaviors comes, not from simple manipulation, but from this linking of cultural symbols and human needs "exclusively" with commodities..[127] What is pathological, Leiss argues, is not the natural state of desiring pleasure, but rather "a pathological state of *the objectification of desire.*" By the latter phrase, Leiss means "the widespread acceptance of grossly exaggerated claims about the importance of such great numbers of commodities for the satisfaction of needs."[128] Needs and wants are socially and historically constructed concepts. What one segment of society calls their needs can, and often have been, defined by others as mere wants. Moreover, as Leiss shows, the stability created by the acceptance of limited needs and wants in traditional cultures has been shattered in our culture, by an excessive desire for an always expanding collection of consumer goods. As Hannah Arendt sums up this transformation, 'the ideals of *homo faber,* the fabricator of the world, which are permanence, stability, and durability, have been sacrificed to abundance, the ideal of the animal laborans."[129]

138

What is pathological, Leiss argues, is, not just that individuals come to identify "feelings of well-being" only with increased consumption of commodities, but the resulting lessening of value placed on the particular qualities of objects, needs, and wants.[130] In sum, the possibilities for human flourishing are restricted to consumer objects, and each particular psychic function is associated with a specific commodity.[131]

In a recent work, Leiss and four of his colleagues have deepened and expanded this analysis of the satisfaction of desire in our consumer culture. They label the manipulationist thesis "black magic."[132] Their analysis of role of advertising in "identity formation" deepens our understanding of the "fluid" nature of consumption, by demonstrating that there is disconnection between the symbolic qualities expressed by commodities and psychological qualities of desire.[133]

This analysis of the ambiguous relationship between desire and satisfaction, created in part at least by our high-consumption society, will prove most useful in succeeding chapters of this book.

The next chapter will examine psychoanalytic writings on what the radical analyst Joel Kovel has called our "neurosis of consumption."[134] It will be seen that their analysis parallels in many ways the social theorists described in this chapter: moving from the biologically determined need and its symbols to our social and existential needs and their signs.

Chapter 3: All-Consuming Desire

There are few things we should keenly desire
if we knew what we wanted.
La Rochefoucauld

It has become the establishment consensus in psychiatry that cognitive-behavioral therapy (CBT), sometimes supplemented by medication, should be the treatment of choice for consumer pathologies.[1] Ironically, this orthodoxy has been more than partly driven by materialist and market influences. The basis of CBT goes back to the central insights about the relationship between our cognitions and our emotions that I have presented above. Also, there can be no doubt that an understanding of certain difficulties with information-processing has advanced the diagnosis and treatment, especially of hoarding disorder. However, this chapter will demonstrate that this emphasis on a narrowly medical model of diagnosis and treatment misses some important insights that come from a more psychodynamic approach to problems of consumption. These insights come from a broader view of the social/cultural forces involved in the development of these disorders, as well as the dynamics behind such strong emotions as fear of loss and threats to personal identity, and "problems in forming emotional attachments."[2] Ever since its inception, Psychoanalysts, especially its European theorists and practitioners, have been willing to see mental health problems within a cultural, economic, and political context. I have argued that only such a contextual and dynamic approach can do justice to the complexity of consumer pathological behavior. It is important to add that, also since its inception, psychoanalysis has not been immune to scientism in its effort to gain and maintain standing in the medical community. Also, there are clear issues regarding cost and class that need to be considered. These are issues that deserve a much more thorough analysis than I have room for here. The main concern of this chapter is a greater understanding of the psychic forces underlying consumer behavior.

Freud's interest in the psychological role of money can be dated as far back as 1898, when in one of his letters to Fliess (letter 82) he wrote: "Happiness is the deferred fulfillment of a prehistoric wish. That is why wealth brings so little happiness; money is not an infantile wish."[3] The issues relating to this early psychoanalysis of money are central to the whole development of Freud's ideas: for example, the roles of 'instinct' (Trieb) and 'symbol', and their interrelationship in society; the whole idea of erotic stages of development; and, most centrally, the concept of 'character' and the technique of 'character analysis' (the latter most closely associated with Wilhelm Reich). Freud's ideas on money evolved from this early remark to a more complex analysis of the "infantile" component in the drive to amass wealth. But Freud was not alone in his interest in the role of money. Most of the leading early psychoanalysts especially Abraham, Ferenczi, Fenichel, and, of course, Reich, made substantive contributions to our understanding of the role money plays in our psychic life.

This chapter, therefore, could not hope to examine all the issues, or all the theorists involved. Instead, after a very brief look at the issue of the relationship of 'instinct' and the symbolic function of money, the chapter will focus primarily on the issue of what psychoanalysis has to say about the way in which the social conditions outlined at the end of chapter 2 are internalized in the development of certain 'character traits'. The importance for psychoanalysis of this last named area of investigation was best summarized by Karl Abraham, when in 1925 he noted that psychoanalysis was concerned, not just with neurotic symptoms, but "pathological deformities of character," which needed to take into consideration the total life of an individual, including social and relational factors. [4]

However, before turning directly to this central concern of dispositions and character formation, it will be necessary to take a brief look at two of the most common critiques of the Freudian approach to psychic reality: (1) the first is a criticism of Freud's general methodology; (2) whereas the second issue has to do with the problematic nature of the instinctual and the symbolic in psychoanalysis, specifically the relationship between these two key concepts as they relate to the psychic role of money. The direct relevance of these issues to the main concern of this chapter will be made apparent in the section on "character traits" which immediately follows this discussion.

One of the most common criticisms of Freud's methodology is that he confuses causal (deterministic) explanation with descriptive (meaningful) understanding.[5] This argument was put

most concisely by MacIntyre (1958) in his book on *The Unconscious*: "One

may ask 'Why?' and expect an answer in terms of reasons, intentions,

purposes and the like; or one may ask 'Why?' and expect an answer in terms

of physiological or psychological determining antecedent

conditions."[6] In its most extreme versions this criticism holds that these two

types of 'why' question are totally incompatible; for instance, that explanations

in terms of unconscious motives can never be equated with causal

explanations.[7] Another version holds that, in his desire to legitimize

psychoanalysis as a natural science, Freud missed the "true" significance of

his discovery as a discipline concerned with intentional acts such as self-

reflection and subjective meanings.[8]

Ludwig Wittgenstein, in his 1931-3 lectures was perhaps the

first to argue that Freud's "real genius" was in describing human nature

and not in giving causal explanations for actions.[9] Since Freud was one of

his favorite authors, no doubt Wittgenstein was aware that Freud himself

states that sometimes he uses key concepts, such as 'unconscious', both in a

descriptive and a causal or dynamic sense; and, that Freud asserts most

unequivocally that it is causal explanation which is the basis of psychoanalysis.[10] But, like most of the other early philosophical critics, Wittgenstein rejected the bulk of Freud's causal theories as unscientific. Frenkel-Brunswik points out that a common important feature of 'dispositions' in psychoanalysis and other sciences is that, like unconscious wishes, they can be present without manifesting themselves.[11]

MacIntyre's position is more respectful of Freud's unique contribution and sophisticated theory. He begins by noting that our *ordinary* explanations of a person's 'intention', 'purpose', 'motive', 'wish' or 'desire' involve both a necessary reference to that individual's actual behavior and, at least the possibility of her avowal of the meaning of that behavior (even if such an avowal requires lengthy psychoanalysis). Human dispositions, as opposed to causal properties of non-human objects, require a reference to both types of explanation "in both the ordinary and Freudian applications of the concepts of motive and intention."[12] Frenkel-Brunswik fails to note this important distinction when she argues that psychoanalytic disposition concepts are the same as concepts such as "magnetism".[13] Benjamin Rubinstein argues that another major difference between psychoanalytic dispositions and purely physical ones is that the former are clearly "hypothetical" or probabilistic — in other words, a person is only more likely to respond in the predicted manner.[14] However, it is clear, MacIntyre maintains, that what Freud was most interested in were those cases which seem to represent counter-examples to this more straightforward model of intentionality; namely, those cases where an individual's behavior (including verbal behavior) seems to run counter to her "likely or professed intentions".[15]

MacIntyre uses the example of a man involved in an unhappy love affair, which he vows to break off, but nonetheless continues to see the woman and to bring her gifts. There are several possible explanations here (including deliberate insincerity), but the one that Freud is most interested in are those cases where an individual "appears unable to recognize a conflict between what he says and what he does".[16] Adolf Grünbaum (following several psychoanalysts, including Freud) argues against those (Habermas in particular) who see the client's avowal of the accuracy of an interpretation as the criterion for a successful analysis. Such avowals are subject to "massive self deceptions," as well as denial. Evidence for the overcoming of repressions involves more than simple avowal. Grünbaum adds that there is strong evidence that we do even have "privileged access" to our conscious motivation, let alone unconscious causes of our behavior.[17] It will be argued further below, that the addictions are clearly cases where an individual's intentions as apparent in her actions are at variance with her avowed intentions as spoken or thought. Grünbaum's critique of psychoanalysis suffers from several deficiencies; but, of particular relevance here is the too hard and fast distinction he draws between ideas and emotions.

Roy Schafer makes a good case for the importance of the defensive use of "disclaimers" of avowed intention, that is, those speech acts where an analysand "disavows responsibility" by "attributing agency" to her "thoughts and impulses."[18] Some might argue that the very concept of 'unconscious motivation' can be misused as such a disclaimer of personal responsibility, for example, in legal proceedings. Once again, the addictions are a place where such 'disclaimers' are commonly utilized, along with other examples of denial. Stuart Hampshire calls these cases of self-deception examples of "concealed dispositions," in order to distinguish them from conscious inclinations (they are "inhibited" or "repressed" dispositions, and they become the basis for the repetition-compulsion, Hampshire maintains.[19]

148

It was precisely to explain such examples of apparent self-deception, R.S. Peters (1960) maintains in his book on *The Concept of Motivation*, which led Freud to postulate the concept of an "unconscious motivation," a concept that introduces *efficient causality* where it is not readily apparent. It should be added that there were other major reasons that led Freud to this concept, such as his experiences with post-hypnotic suggestion.[20] MacIntyre argues that Freud's great insight was to extend the dichotomy between purpose and cause "in a paradoxical fashion, seeing intentions and purposes where the pre-Freudian would have seen only causes, and seeing causes where the pre-Freudian would have seen none..:[21] Peters maintains that the concept of "unconscious wishes" is introduced by Freud to explain situations where "explanation in terms of habits and conscious purpose break down."[22] Peters goes on to argue that "Freud's theory was one of unconscious wishes, not of unconscious reasons."[23] By 'reason' here, Peters seems to mean what MacIntyre refers to as "inner mental planning," something implying consciousness of means and ends; but, also 'reason,' Peters holds, might include physiological effects, character traits or "directed dispositions" like aggressiveness. Whereas, *unconscious wishes*, according to Peters, is a term used by Freud only to refer to physiological effects. Peters (and here MacIntyre agrees) argues that it is precisely here that Freud's "confusion" comes in, for "he tries to treat unconscious motives both as purposes and as causes."[24] The textual justification for this reading (used by Toulmin, Flew and MacIntyre) comes from *The Introductory Lectures on Psychoanalysis,* Lectures 17 & 18. As Flew (1954) reads these lectures, when Freud is being descriptive, and sticking close to the case material, "he talks of finding the motives and purposes of obsessive acts, and of interpreting their meaning."[25] But when Freud switches to the theoretical mode, he talks about natal processes as if they were physical entities which have concrete measurable effects.

In an important and densely packed paper "On the Psychoanalytic Theory of Motivation," the psychologist David Rapaport takes issue with Peters' reading of Freud.[26] Rapaport accepts that "while all behaviors are causally determined, not all causes are motives, and not all behaviors are motivated." But he rejects Peters' equation

150

of motive with reason, and his relegating "not only the physical, chemical, and social effects, but also the effects of instinctual drives, to the category of causes."[27] Peters wishes to show that not all behaviors are caused by drives, that some actions are "motivated by 'reasons' involving social rules."[28] However, in insisting that instinctual drives are only causes and not motives, Peters takes too narrow a view of both causes and reasons; and he ignores the fact that behaviors are often overdetermined ('overdetermination' will be examined later in this chapter). As Rapaport defines instinctual drives, they include, not only the passive and compulsive character of causal factors, but also the "purposive directionality" which is characteristic of 'rule-following' behaviors, and other 'motives'. Rapaport defines 'motives' as *appetitive forces* with four characteristics: (1) *Peremptoriness* or a "mandatory character"; (2) a *"Cyclic character"* in which their peremptoriness increases and decreases with "consummation" followed by increased compulsion; (3) *"Selectiveness"* — that is "the direction of the motive force" is determined by the "object" and "the path by which the object is obtainable"; and (4) *"Displaceability"*— other objects related in some way to the object of a motive can become its substitute.[29]

These categories, of course, are closely related to the four different aspects of Freud's concept of *instinct*.[30]

Before turning directly to the passages from Freud's *Lectures* which are the basis of Peters' attack, it is necessary to take a brief look at Freud's theory of causality, which, from the very beginning of his career, turns out to also be much more complex than his critics seem to realize. In "A Reply to Criticisms of My Paper on Anxiety Neurosis", Freud answers those who argue that he confuses the "psychic derivation" of anxiety with his own physical causation by "sexual noxiae."[31] The first important point that Freud makes here is the overdetermined nature of such causes (*aiberdeterminiert* is used, in the sense of "several factors" acting in conjunction).[32] This term itself, it might be argued, carries with it the confusion of *cause* and *meaning* in that it is used here to refer to multiple causes and used elsewhere (e.g., Freud, 1900) to refer to a series of meanings.[33] However, what Freud means here by factors is something much more complex than this criticism understands. First of all, what can be overdetermined includes traumatic events,' symptoms, as well as meanings in the sense of interpretation (*Deutungen*) and symbols in dreams.[34] What is more,

Freud offers a more sophisticated theory of causality, with four different varieties, each of which needs to be taken into consideration: (1) preconditions (*Bedingungen* — literally, stipulations) — either innate or acquired dispositions; (2) specific causes (*specifische Urzache* — this last word carries the connotation of origin or source) — these are sufficient conditions (though they require, of course, preconditions), in that they are "never absent when the effects actually take place" and they suffice "in the required quantity or intensity, to bring about the effect"; (3) Contributory causes — the adjective carries a meaning of concurrent and competitive) — these are neither necessary nor-sufficient to produce the effect alone, but they "cooperate with" (the sense of the German is more literally "when added to") the other causes to bring about the effect (this is where the social "nourishing" items of chapter 2 above come into play); and, finally; (4) the exciting or releasing (redemptive) cause — the immediate precipitating cause or the final cause in the sequence.

Freud's primary concern in this "Reply to Critics" was to argue against the view that hereditary predisposition alone, without the other causal factors (particularly sexual noxiae as *specific causes*) can account for the neuroses. However, when one examines the various causal factors which he introduced throughout his writings, one again notes, not only the complexity of his view of science, but particularly the blending of intentional and efficient causes and mental factors. Freud clearly saw not only physical forces as causal agents, but mental forces as well. Many of the critics of Freud examined at the beginning of this chapter attempt to distinguish between the so-called early Freud, who presumably used mechanical and deterministic explanations, and a later Freud, who, though never totally abandoning explanations in terms of such causal factors, nevertheless introduced intentional concepts as parallel understanding. However, when one looks more deeply into Freud's early works, a number of concepts appear to go well beyond the purely mechanical. To mention only two: (1) purposive ideas —*Zielvorstellung* (*Ziel* carries meanings of goal, end or objective and *Vorstellung,* which Freud borrowed from German idealist philosophy, means 'representation', as well as mental image; and, (2) unconscious fantasy, which as Laplanche & Pontalis point out, refers to the whole "world of the imagination," rather than "the faculty of imagining."[35] And, when one examines Freud's last published work (Freud, 1941) his evolutionary and biological foundations are still very clearly apparent throughout. Steven Goldberg shows how Freud's early works also include many intentional elements similar to those of the so-called late Freud.[36]

Before concluding this section, it will help to further clarify what *is not* being argued, if I take a very brief look at some works on Freud which go too far, either in the direction of trying to "humanize" him (by down-playing his clearly scientific foundations), or in playing down the important role of 'intentional' concepts in his work. The first work is a small book by Bruno Bettleheim (1983). Bettleheim demonstrates persuasively that many of the standard English renderings of key German terms in Freud have the effect of making these concepts sound mechanical and abstract by ignoring the intentional connotations in the original. Freud clearly had a penchant for adopting common German words for his own uses.[37] For example, Freud describes the German word *Verdrangung* (commonly translated as "repression"), as the "cornerstone," "most essential part," and *"sine qua non"* of psychoanalysis.[38] Bettleheim notes that the original carries the connotation of "a strong inner motive or urge."[39] An equally important term, and perhaps the one which has been most misleadingly translated, is *Trieb,* usually rendered as "instinct' (although Goldberg's example of

Seele "soul" as "psychic apparatus" would be a close contender).[40] Bettleheim notes that the original German comes closer to "impulse" — "an impelling force; a sudden inclination to act, without conscious thought; a motive or tendency coming from within."[41] Examples like these could be multiplied, and this book has added a few new ones to Bettleheim's. However, the conclusions which Bettleheim draws from his exegesis sets up two false dichotomies: (1) the early Freud versus late Freud reading, that is, the early scientist who later became a humanist (Bettleheim, 1983, p. 32); and (2) the natural sciences (*Naturwissenschaften*) versus humanistic sciences (*Geisteswissenschaften*) dichotomy — that is, the view that there are two very different types of science, one for natural objects and one for the study of man.[42] One passage, written as late as 1933 will serve to show the falseness of both views.[43] For here, in a relatively late work, Freud makes it very clear (as he does again in several other late works, for example, Freud, 1925) his strong and unequivocal allegiance to one view of science; one in which the logic of science is basically the same as other forms of reasoning (this Lecture, in Freud, 1933, also includes a statement about the importance of psychological factors in economic behavior and the cultural differences in these behaviors).[44]

Another psychoanalyst who very early on rejected the view that psychoanalysis is a branch of *Geisteswissenschaften* and, therefore, a discipline which deals with meaningful connections as opposed to causal explanations, was Heinz Hartmann. In an essay on "Understanding and Explanation" he argues against the "hermeneutic version" (Grünbaum's term) over thirty years before that reading of Freud had received its canonical formulation.[45] Hartmann's main concerns in this very interesting essay are to demonstrate the limits of a purely phenomenological or descriptive approach to psychology and to argue that psychoanalysis deals with causal explanations, albeit with a more complex theory of causality. Hartmann admits that psychoanalysis, "to a far greater degree than other schools of scientific psychology," deals "with psychological connections that are also understandable."[46] However, Hartmann argues that psychoanalysis goes beyond the mere description of intentional acts or states by offering explanations and constructing hypotheses that are "from the causal point of view."[47] Hartmann draws a distinction between the phenomena that psychoanalysis attempts to describe,

157

which are capable of being experienced with "sympathetic understanding" (*Nacherleben* means to "attempt to reproduce in one's own experience what someone else has experienced"), and the methodological "goal of psychoanalysis" that is causal explanation.[48] What is more, the kind of causal explanation introduced by psychoanalysis recognizes effects which proceed, not only from the physical to the mental, but also from the mental to the mental.[49] Psychoanalysis, as a science, needs to be concerned with the validation of both types of causal connection; and 'empathic understanding' alone cannot verify such relations. Subjective 'meaning-connections' cannot be self-evident, Hartmann points out, because of the very phenomena of self-deception discovered by psychoanalysis (and described above in the discussion of MacIntyre and behaviors which, like the addictive, run counter to avowed intentions). Hartmann notes that a good deal of our behavior is *unintentional* in the "usual sense" of lacking a conscious instrumentality or goal-directedness. Of course, Freud's great achievement was to expand on that usual sense; in the words of MacIntyre: "he alters completely the boundary between the intelligible and the unintelligible."[50] It was in *The Psychopathology of Everyday Life* that Freud was, perhaps, clearest about this goal of demonstrating how "unintentional performances" have "valid" and "determining motives."[51] Of course, Freud's achievement was also to expand our notion of the 'intentional' as well. He took over the idea of the mind as 'intentional', (i.e., an amalgam of purposive mental states directed towards objects by means of representations) from his teacher Franz Brentano.[52] However, Freud's great contribution was to introduce a whole new category of intentional entities which, though likewise directed toward objects, were not accessible to conscious reflection. And "it is these unconscious representations which motivate us."[53] These unconscious representations do have *meaning*, in the sense of functional purpose.[54] In the provocative words of Philip Rieff, "Freud detected meaning in everything," while at the same time reacting to what he saw as "the overvaluation" of our rationality.[55]

Hartmann's comments about the nature of the phenomena examined by psychoanalysis brings to mind two explanations for why Freud needed to expand existing psychological methods: First, there is the purely logical requirement that a theoretical model must be richer or more powerful than the explanandum, in order for the explanandum to be subsumable under comprehensive general principles; and, second, as Robert Paul Wolff notes, only an equally rich and complex language could possibly describe the "complex, many-layered" forms of self-deception and unconscious mechanisms proposed by psychoanalysis.[56]

Even though Freud used words and concepts already in common parlance, as Stephen Toulmin points out, "their incorporation into theory involves some change in meaning or a *language shift*."[57]

It is this relationship between common and transformed meaning which Lacan described as "dialectical."[58] It is also part of the basis of Freud's concept of over-determination.[59] Just as the individual is an amalgam of social, cultural and economic influences (like those described briefly in chapter 1 above), so are her immediate behavior, symptoms and unconscious symbols "a plurality of determining factors" which give meaning to her actions.[60] It is part of the argument of this book that complex behaviors, like pleonexia, cannot be understood in any other way. David Rapaport, suggests that even behaviors which appear to be the result of "nonmotivational causes" have present "highly

neutralized derivative motivations or motivations of little actual effect."[61]

However, as Hartmann notes, it is precisely in the area of

complex character or personality traits that we need causal

explanations that go beyond subjective evidence (*Evidenz* as used here is close

to our introspection), and can account for personal and interpersonal

deception.[62] Here one is dealing with complex motives not apparent to the

casual observer and actor alike. There are two areas, Hartmann asserts, in

which psychology needs to proceed beyond the limitations of

sympathetic experience (*Nacherleben*): the first, as already noted, is

unconscious motivational processes; and, the other is "somatic intrusion."

By the latter term, Hartmann means the influence of somatic states on

moods, feelings and actions, and he assumes a principle of "universal

psychophysical parallelism."[63] But here Hartmann goes too far in the

direction of a *simplistic* mechanical reductionism for Freud. Once again,

Freud's position is more complicated (too complicated to go into much

detail here). Suffice it to say, that, although Freud did maintain a

psychophysical dualism of sorts at other times he, also, specifically

rejected "psychophysical parallelism" as having "insoluble

difficulties" (*unlösbaren Schwierigkeiten* —the latter term also means obstacles.[64] Freud notes that, since we are totally ignorant of such somatic causes, it would prematurely close off debate to involve them. Elsewhere Freud notes that "an instinct appears to us as a concept on the frontier between the mental and the somatic, as the physical representative of the stimuli originating from within the organism and reaching the mind, as a measure of the demand made upon the mind for work in consequence of its connection with the body."[65]

What is more important for this book is the fact that, as has been noted throughout this chapter, the "intentional categories — ideas, purposes, resolutions and so forth" are the "latent mental processes" involved in unconscious activities.[66] Hartmann, himself, goes on to note that psychoanalysis utilizes "psychological concepts where previously explanations would have been based solely on physiological processes."[67] What is involved here is another type of understanding, an unconscious type, one which is overdetermined by a number of different factors.[68] Hartmann states that "in this extended sense of understanding, assumptions are made about the presence of certain mental states on the basis of knowledge of other understandable connections, and these assumptions make understanding possible."[69] The example Hartmann puts forth is one of particular interest to this book; namely, the transition from anal eroticism to avarice (as will be seen shortly, this transition involves all four of Freud's types of causality). However, Hartmann's main concern is that an approach to the mind based on 'understanding' can degenerate into purely linguistic arguments about symbols and meanings; and, that such an approach cannot hope to answer questions about what he calls somatic intrusions. What is more, Hartmann expounds what he believes is a more scientific, "value free," methodology for psychoanalysis, an impossible position which he himself was to modify greatly over thirty years later.[70] But what is more important for this book are Hartmann's concluding remarks about the expanded view of causal explanation in Freud's work. On the one hand, Hartmann correctly notes that the basic motivational terms of Freud's theory were not intentions and purposes, but instinctual drives or impulses. It is true that despite many successive revisions of his instinct theory, it clearly remained rooted in law-like generalizations of a biological nature.[71] On the other hand, Hartmann (like MacIntyre and Peters above) recognizes that Freud was often careless when drawing this important distinction between meaningful and causally determined in his writings. Hartmann reiterates that that was because the factors being investigated are of intentional nature (he uses the term teleological); and, that these factors are assigned a meaningful relationship to other factors of the mind.[72] Like Griinbaum, Hartmann maintains that the connections between these meaningful or purposeful factors can and need to be verified empirically. However, Hartmann also recognizes that the type of causal explanations utilized by psychoanalysis includes teleological interpretation.[73] In fact Freud states that a "basic pillar" of psychoanalysis is his theorem that "when conscious purposive ideas are abandoned, concealed purposive ideas assume control of the currents of ideas."[74] Marshall Edelson offers a very interesting analysis of the importance of purposive interpretations in psychoanalysis, one which also recognizes the complexity of Freud's principles of causality.[75]

Grünbaum's extensive and sophisticated contribution to this debate can only be touched upon here in those areas where it directly relates to the concerns of this book. His main concern in his critique of the "hermeneutic version" is to argue against the "pernicious myth that, precisely insofar as explanations in psychoanalysis are indeed motivational or supply unconscious 'reasons' for our actions, they cannot be a particular *species* of causal explanations."[76] These hermeneutic interpreters of psychoanalysis misinterpret not only Freud's complex causal theory, but his theory of "meaning" and "purpose" as well. Grünbaum makes two different forms of critique against the authors he examines: the first is exegetical — that is, that their reading of Freud is in error; the second is to show errors in their logic or philosophy of science. It is easiest for Grünbaum to demonstrate that Freud did not see his work in the way these authors characterize it; much more difficult to show that his causal arguments are the same as those in any other science. Following Robert Shope's careful and exhaustive reading of Freud's various uses of the term 'meaning' *Bedeutung* or 'significance' and *Sinn* (which can be translated 'disposition'), Grünbaum is able to show that such mental phenomena as "dreams, symptoms or parapraxes" have "meaning" for Freud as *signs* which are stand-ins for unconscious desires, rather than *symbols* which stand *for* the (content of) the wish in the sense of referring to it.[77] Grünbaum's critique of hermeneutic logic derives from what he characterizes as the "reasons *versus* causes" thesis.[78] This is the thesis (already examined earlier in this chapter) which holds that a person's reasons for her actions cannot be a cause of these same actions. Grünbaum first notes that Freud firmly rejected this dichotomy, since he deemed explanatory reasons to be a species of motive, and motives, whether conscious or unconscious, to be a species of the genus cause. Moreover, he *allowed* that some motives might not even be mental. Thus, he characterizes the psychoanalyst's quest for sufficient motives as a refined implementation of our 'innate craving for causality.'"[79]

However, looking at the original passages quoted here by Grünbaum, it is apparent that Freud does refer to both the causal and intentional use of motive. First, in the passage just before this one, he refers to how "symptoms and chance acts express" both "impulses *and also* purposes."[80] And in the passage quoted by Grünbaum, after noting that for psychoanalysis there is "nothing trifling, arbitrary or fortuitous" in mental life, and the broadening of the concept of motivation (noted earlier in this chapter), Freud specifically refers to the "manifold motivation" of these "psychic effects," disagreeing with the view that "our alleged inborn causal need is explained satisfactorily by a single psychic cause or motive."[81] Grünbaum (and Shope) are correct, however, when they maintain that Freud's *primary* use of the term motive is the etymological one of that which "instigates" or "moves us to action."[82]

The relevance of this debate to the main concern of this chapter can best be seen by turning briefly to a few comments by the early exponent of the reasons vs. causes thesis.[83] Ludwig Binswanger argued for an existentialist critique of Freud's derivation of the character trait of miserliness from infantile anal eroticism. First, he maintains that "psychoanalysis saw in a character trait such as miserliness an 'unintelligible basic motive [*Befindlichkeitsmoment*],' that is to say a purely irrational manifestation."[84] Binswanger's point, according to Gerald Izenberg, is that, despite some suggestive literary allusions, Freud is unable to demonstrate any "subjectively meaningful connection" between gold and feces.[85] What's even more important, I would argue, is the history of how this supposed explanation of hoarding behavior was put to use for anti-Semitic propaganda.[86] Binswanger accepts the connection, Izenberg maintains, but argues that "what made the equation possible *for the* subject was the common denominator in both activities of filling up an emptiness."[87] In Binswanger's interpretation it is not the infant's retention of feces that is the "*cause or the motive*," but rather the "common denominator" is this filling of a void, and this is what is essential for understanding the hoarding of money.[88] What is interesting here is the possibility of linking disorders of acquisition with hoarding disorder as having a common unconscious motive of filling a sense of emptiness.

Izenberg argues that Binswanger's "equivocation between 'cause' and 'motive'" here is a recognition on his part "of the peculiar logical structure of psychoanalytic explanation."[89] In other words, the true meaning of the connection between the character trait and the retention of feces is not to be found in a physical impulse, "but the defense against the feeling of emptiness or the danger of losing something that was vital to the integrity of the self."[90] That this is a radical departure from Freud's theory can be seen by turning to his 1908 essay on "Character and Anal Eroticism."[91] Freud begins the essay by referring to the "organic connection" between the type of character and the behavior of an organ; and adds "that no theoretical anticipation played any part in that impression."[92] His first inference is one about genetic predisposition of "exceptionally strong accentuation of erotogenicity of anal zone."[93] Freud had introduced most of these ideas, using the German word *Anlage* — disposition in sense of 'natural tendency but also talent.[94] The key process in the movement from this predisposition to the dispositional traits of "orderliness, frugality and obstinacy" is "the diversion or deflection" of the "sexual goal or aim" to other purposes — namely, the process of "sublimation" *Sublimierung*[95] As noted by Laplanche & Pontalis, the term sublimation, not only blends purpose with mechanism, as can be seen in the passage just quoted, it also combines the art-criticism concept of the sublime with the scientific concept of a chemical process, i.e., passage from a solid to a gaseous state.[96] In a later essay on "The Disposition to Obsessional Neurosis" Freud adds the important defense of "reaction-formation" to sublimation as the processes that, when generalized, can lead to character-traits.[97] It is important to note that the reaction-formations are particularly active in anal characters and in obsessive traits.[98] Otto Fenichel notes that reaction-formations make for "a 'once-and-for-all', definitive change of the personality." In other words, this defense becomes a habitual part of the individual's personality structure in anticipation of future danger, rather than a reaction to an instinctual danger in the present.[99]

Finally, following his daughter's codification of *The Ego and the Mechanisms of Defense*, Freud expanded on his concept of the "modification or alteration of the I or Ego" *Ichveranderung*.[100] Anna Freud had been influenced by Wilhelm Reich's concept of the "armor-plating of character" (*Charakterpanzerung*) or what she calls the "permanent defense phenomena."[101] Such character-traits as "arrogant behavior," Anna Freud maintains, are "residues of very vigorous defensive processes in the past."[102] The problem for psychoanalysis as a form of treatment for consumer pathologies is that such "modes of defense" become, in the words of Sigmund Freud, "fixated in the ego"; and, are, thereby, not subject to the same forms of manipulation (whether from internal or external desires and temptations).[103] And, therefore, these dispositions are particularly intractable to treatment. In his essay on "Analysis Terminable and Interminable" Freud acknowledges two different types of disposition, depending on their mode of origin: the first are those individual tendencies that a person is born with (her particular constitution); and the second are those acquired "modifications of the I," which can come from accidental trauma or from the course of development.[104] Freud's Lamarckian ideas about inheritance tend to muddy the distinction here, but it is clear also from Freud, 1913, that these are basically two separate but related categories; or, to be more specific, two poles of a continuum. So here, toward the very end of his career, Freud returns to the complexity of causality and etiology which was examined earlier in this chapter in Freud, 1895.[105] Only now there is a certain pessimism for the outcome of treatment, given not only the "constitutional strength of instinct" but also given the possibility of "an unfavourable modification of the ego in the defensive conflict" (*die im Abwehrkampf erworbene ungünstige Veränderung des Ichs*).[106] Freud further notes that, "the stronger the constitutional factor the more readily will a trauma lead to fixation, with its sequel in a disturbance of development; the stronger the trauma the more certain it is that it will have injurious effects even when the patient's instinctual life is normal."[107]

What Freud means here by the conflict of the instinctual and defensive factors is further analyzed by Rapaport, under his definition of 'motives' as "appetitive internal forces"; except that for Freud, at least in the case of modification of the ego, *social pressures do play a significant role*.[108] In the case of instinctual forces, Rapaport is correct to point out that the individual experiences such motives as "compulsions", which are often "ego-dystonic instinctual impulses," and against which the ego takes up a defensive attitude.[109] However, as Freud notes, the ego, in part at least, treats these "instinctual demands ... like external forces... because it understands that satisfaction of instincts would lead to conflicts with the external world."[110] This conflict is described by Freud in a number of other places.[111] It is the origin, among other things, of the important process of 'substitute gratification or satisfaction; a concept important, not only to symptom formation, but to character formation as well.[112] This process also plays an important function in formation of pleonexia, as will be seen below. As Philip Rieff states, in his usual colorful prose, Freud's mature view of man can be characterized as the conflict between "two objective forces — unregenerate instincts and overbearing culture."[113]

To a large extent this battle gets played out in a struggle between the instinctual and the symbolic; for example, in his article on "Repression," Freud notes that it is the 'ideational representatives' of the instincts that gets repressed.[114] A person's character, on this reading of Freud, becomes the individualized way in which she resolves this

172

conflict. To quote Rieff once again: "since the individual can neither extirpate his instincts nor wholly reject the demands of society, his character expresses the way in which he organizes and appeases the conflict between the two."[115] Erich Fromm put it succinctly, when he called *character* "a solution forged over time."[116] Daniel Yankelovich and my great teacher, William Barrett noted that "conflict is probably the key notion throughout all Freud's thinking;" adding that "Erich Erikson stated that psychoanalysis is the view of man as conflict."[117] Roy Schafer (1989) argued that Kohut is the one exception to this rule.

However, at least two issues arise if one is to maintain this view of character formation: (1) First, it is clearly the case, as noted earlier, that 'modes of defense' may be maintained even when the conflict underlying them has long since become quiescent; (2) but, more important for purposes here, it is clear from the kind of evidence put forth in chapter 2 above, that some types of dispositions to behavior are nourished by a particular society rather than being the result of such conflict.

One psychoanalyst who dealt with some of these issues of the relationship between the development of character and the influence of society, specifically as it relates to what I've called pleonexia, was Otto

Fenichel. As Russell Jacoby notes, Fenichel accepted the view that

"history stamps neurosis with its insignia." But, he also took exception to the

reduction of culture to merely sexual character types.[118] In fact, Fenichel

rejected any form of reductionism, including the biological variety, as

well as what he called "culturalism." Fenichel basically accepted the

formulation of a conflict between the instincts and external

social constraints as outlined above. He was particularly

concerned that the social psychoanalysts (the Neo-Freudians) were

giving up too many of the key insights from instinct theory.[119]

Fenichel begins his important essay on "The Drive to Amass Wealth" by

affirming the existence of a specific instinct to strive for wealth, with

an active aspect of "acquisitiveness" and a passive function of "being

supported on an oral level."[120] At first glance this would appear to be an

example of the kind of circular and vacuous use of the instinct concept

criticized by Frenkel-Brunswik.[121] In her critical view, creation of a

specific instinct for "every variety of manifest behavior" renders the

concept of instinct in a purely descriptive and "superfluous" role

from the point of view of causal explanation. The concept of instinct

174

is supposed to bridge the gap between explanations in terms of causes and effects and explanations in terms of intentions and purposes, but fails to perform this task when confined to such a purely descriptive role. The problem is one central to the methodological difficulties of biological reductionism, which commits a *petitio principi* by pushing back the causal question to the innate level (this would appear to be, in part, Borneman's criticism, alluded to above, of Ferenczi's "Capitalistic instinct" as an "unfortunate terminus technicus."[122]. However, this is not Fenichel's understanding of the drive to amass wealth. First, because he notes, (following Freud 1926) that such "highly specialized" instincts allow further reduction to a "source" in more "primal instincts."[123] Freud distinguished between an instinct's "impetus, its aim, its object and its source" (parenthetically, the term *Triebschicksale,* translated as "Vicissitudes" in the English title of this essay, carries the teleological meaning of entelechy and fate).[124] In Freud's last book, after noting that one can distinguish "an indeterminate number" of instincts, Freud goes on to further note that "instincts can change their aim (by displacement)" and can even replace one another.[125]

However, even more importantly, for both Freud and Fenichel (and this book), both the specific aims and the objects of our instincts are largely socially determined (it is not possible here to trace the complex transformations of these terms in Freud's writings).[126] Fenichel argues that "biological facts are modified by social facts." Freud notes that the child has only the concept of a "present or gift" *Geschenk* which only with age and social circumstances gets replaced by "money."[127] Fenichel goes further in this direction of seeing the influence of the social on instincts than Freud does, however; for he argues that, not only the specific goal of accumulating *money* but the whole drive of acquisitiveness is, in part at least, socially determined.[128]

In fact, Fenichel introduces an important issue: if a particular behavior is considered "rational" in a given society, such that its absence as a motivating influence would be considered a manifestation of *abnormality,* how then is it possible to consider that behavior to be a form of illness. After all, in a society such as ours, it is a "rational motive" to believe "that the more money one possesses, the better one can satisfy one's needs."[129] Of course, this is not a problem which is peculiar to the pleonexic. Freud was constantly reminding us that the boundary

176

between the normal and abnormal is a "fluid" one.[130] And this was particularly true in the case of "character anomalies," which are "subtle and most often experienced without pain, and anxiety or displeasure" and are "rationalized away with terms such as 'it's his nature.'"[131] Though this issue is common to a number of psychoanalytic categories of psychopathology, it is, nevertheless, particularly pronounced in the area of this study. In her excellent book, *The problem of human needs and the critique of civilization*, Patricia Springborg notes how this problem is related to Marcuse's concern that people, far from feeling alienated in advanced capitalist society, actually "recognize themselves in their commodities." She adds that Marcuse is concerned with how what he considers to be "false needs" get *introjected*.[132] This concept of true/false needs, which I criticized earlier in this book, receives some weak or putative foundation in Freud's idea of "innate needs" — *mitgebrachten Bedurfnisse* — literally needs that come with the organism.[133] However, Freud's concept is better understood as an example of what Joel Marks calls a "dispositional desire," for example "the desire to run away when threatened", which is a state rather than an event.[134] Desires that arise from events or situations Marks calls, "occurrent desires."[135]

A partial response to this issue will involve some of the same methodological points made earlier in this chapter. The first thing to note is that: there are two conditions which are usually associated with psychopathology: (1) feeling distress in situations which normally ought not to be distress producing, and (2) maladaptive behavior. In most cases both conditions are present, but either may be present without the other.[136] In the case of pleonexia, depending, on the financial position of the patient, distress over her compulsive spending may or may not be present; but, in all but the rarest of cases, such behavior can be considered maladaptive. In addition, there are also times when one's needs or desires take an intentional state as their object, such as when an addicted person desires to *cease to desire* to shop.[137] Also, of course, the examples of an individual who acts contrary to her professed desire, which were seen earlier to be basic to the psychoanalytic view of pathology, can mean that feelings of distress are absent in situations which normally ought to be stress producing (a situation not necessarily accounted for in philosopher Kaikhosov Irani's criteria; although it would probably be considered part of the definition of 'maladaptive behavior' to be examined shortly). Irani notes that both his

178

criteria of psychopathology presuppose intentions and purposes: in the first case through "feelings" and other such states of consciousness; and in the second, the very "notion of adaptation implies the notions of function and purpose."[138]

How then is maladaptive behavior, such as pleonexia, defined by psychoanalysis? Irani recognizes two separate types of explanation which both involve intentional states (his analysis basically summarizes views already covered earlier in this chapter) : the first is the case in which an overt act B differs from an avowed or intended act A because a conscious motive G differs from an unconscious motive W' (here it is necessary that the individual have at least one *unconscious* motive; two conscious, though conflicted, motives would not count as a psychoanalytic explanation for a maladaptive act). The second explanation involves the introduction of defense mechanisms and character traits. Here what is postulated are certain: Unconscious states, S, which for one reason or another cannot be manifested in behavior, and which have generated a set of attitudes or dispositions, D, characterized by wants and styles of behavior. The overt act, B, must now be interpreted as the behavior of an individual with G having an attitudinal and dispositional set D', and which, without D', may have led to act A.[139] Irani goes on to note that defense mechanisms are "much more likely to alter the motives rather than just the act"; thereby introducing another set of goals; and the overt act would then be considered an appropriate implementation of these goals. Of course, a lot is left out of this description: for example, it says nothing about the key issue of how these "unconscious states, attitudes or dispositions" get their original formation. What is missing, in part is any notion of primary and secondary dispositions, such as Stuart Hampshire provides. At every stage in life new dispositions or inclinations to respond in certain ways to certain situations are being formed. The contribution of psychoanalysis is to show how these new or "secondary dispositions can be traced back to unconscious memories of primitive satisfactions and frustrations of instinctual needs, modified by complicated processes of repression, projection, displacement, transference, and so on."[140] Also, the question as to whether our wants and desires are merely preferences we freely choose, or whether they are conventions imposed by the culture we live in, is not simply of psychological importance, but it has profound political implications as well.

One final point needs to be made on this issue of 'abnormality' and pleonexia, before returning to Fenichel's essay. It was noted earlier that one of the key defenses involved in the formation of character traits (especially of the compulsive inclinations) is reaction-formation. From the very first introduction of the concept of this defense (in Freud, 1905, p. 78f) Freud noted its importance for normal development. However, Freud also notes that such normal traits of character can become exaggerated and can take on "the force of a symptom," as in the compulsive neurotic.[141] So once again, it can be seen that the normal/abnormal dispositions are more like a continuum than hard and separate categories.

Returning to Fenichel's important essay on "The Drive to Amass Wealth," there are three "irrational" forces which he argues lie "behind" the rational reasons to "accumulate possessions." For the first of these, he borrows a phrase from Nietzsche and Adler, namely, "the will to power." Adler was interested in the question of what determines healthy adaptation to the environment, as well as the dispositional factors which impede such adaptations. He postulated a natural striving for mastery and better adaptation.[142] Adler was also strongly interested in the social and political determinants of adaptation.[143] However, he was strongly criticized by other psychoanalysts with this same interest — for example, Wilhelm Reich— for his overemphasis on the teleological concept of aim, rather than the causal factor of instincts, as well as his conservative emphasis on adaptation to current social conditions.[144] The "will to power" was seen as a neurotic response to feelings of insecurity rather than the universal human trait which Nietzsche assumed.[145] The term 'power' is defined broadly by Fenichel to include what he calls here and elsewhere "narcissistic needs," in particular the need for "self-regard" or "self-esteem."[146] Here Fenichel acknowledges ego and interpersonal motivations of equal importance to "the instinctual requirements of the id."[147] The obverse of this "will to power" is "pathological fear of impoverishment" because the "loss of love and of possessions that is feared means always a loss of self-regard, a diminution of power."[148] The connection between self-regard and power is a social one, Fenichel maintains, based on the honor and power which is bestowed upon the rich in our society. But it also has its basis in the infant's feelings of omnipotence, which are dependent on satisfaction of the "primal desire" for food.

Fenichel was influenced here by Sandor Rado, who attempted to explain both the effects and the causes of addiction to drugs in terms of what he called "meta-erotism."[149] Rado's greatest contribution to the study of addiction was probably his observation that addicts have a low frustration level when it comes to gratification, something he called "tense depression." Rado noted a tendency to regression to a pregenital level in the addict, a "turning away from real [i.e., genital] love-objects." He noted, following Freud (1904) and Abraham (1924), the very strong oral component to "the flight into morbid craving", as well as the links with mania and melancholia.[150] This kind of reductionist analysis in terms of sexuality has justly given psychoanalysis its bad reputation. However, Fenichel makes good use of Freud, Abraham, and Rado. In the view of Fenichel, money serves to supply the individual with her quota of self-regard in a manner analogous to how food relieves the infant's hunger. The equation between riches and power and respect in our society is why "the original instinctual aim is not for riches" but these narcissistic needs.[151]

The second of the "irrational" motives for the drive to amass riches is a generic "collecting instinct", so that the former drive is a subdivision of a more basic acquisitive instinct. This more general "desire to possess" is a "direct expression of the narcissistic need to enlarge as much as possible the compass of one's own ego."[152] How does this differ from the first narcissistic need (i.e., self-respect)? What is involved here is a somatic notion; that is, the bodily expansion of the ego through possession (first of all, of clothing).[153] This reductionistic concept of "bodily narcissism" with its emphasis on "overcompensation" related to castration fears is highly problematic.[154] These "fears of bodily injury" become associated with the loss of money through the familiar money equals feces equation. However, Fenichel criticizes the more extreme exponents of this view (e.g., Ferenczi) who maintain that money was "expressly invented for the purpose of satisfying" the anal instinct (one is reminded of Voltaire's satirical remark about those who maintained that the nose was intended for the purpose of holding glasses). Fenichel states that this is an unwarranted "extrapolation to phylogenesis from ontogenetic data", for our social system, for its own political purposes, simply appropriates this erogenous pleasure in collecting to strengthen its hold on economic conditions. Fenichel makes a very important point when he notes that "not only the unconscious attitude toward feces but also the attitude toward introjections of every kind can be projected onto money."[155] I soon learned, as a couples therapist, that money issues are a symbolic substitute for other conflicts. One example which Fenichel uses, one which adumbrates a number of recent insights from feminist theory, is of women whose striving for money (one could add for possessions in general) is, at least in part, a compensation for "a whole series of introjected objects that have been withheld from them."[156] The notion of introjected objects was used by Abraham, in an important essay to explain the "positive and negative narcissism" of the manic-depressive.[157] Following Freud's insight that the melancholic introjects the lost love-object, Abraham notes that the self-reproaches and lack of self-regard of the depressive phase "emanates from this introjected object."[158] Abraham's insights about the manic phase, in this essay and elsewhere, will prove important when it comes to differentiating pleonexia from this disorder.[159] Fenichel offers another example, that of men who identify money with "their potency [and] who experience any loss of money as a castration." His final example is those impulsive individuals: who — according to their attitude of the moment toward taking, giving, or withholding — accumulate or spend money, or alternate between accumulation and spending, quite impulsively, without regard for the real significance of money, and often to their own detriment (sometimes unconsciously desired).[160]

The last of the four factors which Fenichel sees as having an effect on acquisitiveness he labels "the sociological source." Although instincts represent general tendencies, Fenichel argues that the "specific form" which such tendencies can assume depends upon "certain definite social conditions" being in place; in this case a capitalist economy of commodities.[161] Given the overdetermination of human motives and actions, the problem is to learn to distinguish what is primary from motives that are situational.[162] Fenichel would appear to answer this question in favor of social forces; for he believes that even such biological structures as anal-erotism depend "to a large extent upon social factors."[163] Once social institutions are in place, at least, they have direct effects on our instinctual life. The separate question of how these specific institutions come about, Fenichel asserts, can only be answered after detailed anthropological *and* historical investigations (such as those sketched in chapter 2).[164] However, Fenichel's real answer is to

186

oppose the notion of a single determining force or set of forces: only through the "continual reciprocal action" of specific social and instinctual needs, under specific historical, as well as economic conditions, could give rise to a drive to amass wealth.

The psychoanalyst who made the most concerted effort (at least in his early writings) to understand this reciprocal action of biological, social and political factors on character development was Wilhelm Reich. There is room here only to briefly look at how his early (pre-1935) ideas can shed some light on the etiology and differentiation of pleonexia. According to Russell Jacoby, Fenichel and Reich, despite their common concern with social and political influences on character, parted company partly because of what Fenichel considered Reich's "sexual reductionism" and "romanticism", as well as his failure "to understand Marxism."[165] Reich, however, did "reject eclectic attempts to combine 'instinct' and 'economy' arbitrarily" holding that the child of these parents was "more than the sum total of his parents"; and, he also rejected what he called "vulgar Marxism"; arguably no psychoanalyst has been more misrepresented in his ideas than Reich.[166] A classic example can be found in Yiannis Gabriel, where she argues that he left out of his synthesis of Freud and Marx "the one common ingredient of the two original theories, conflict."[167] Nothing could be further from the truth, as can be seen repeatedly in Reich, where conflict plays a major role.[168] What is true, however, as Michael Schneider points out, is that Reich believed, unlike Freud or Marx, in a "natural sociability," a "capacity for love," and "spontaneous joy in work" which was simply perverted by social repression. Schneider argues convincingly that Reich lost some of the subtleties of Freud's instinct theory which I have examined above.[169]

In fact, there are a number of points of contact between Fenichel and Reich: for one thing, though it was seen earlier that Reich rejected Adler's emphasis on the purposeful to the neglect of the biological, nonetheless, like Fenichel, Reich also rejected the notion of capitalism springing whole cloth from the instincts; in addition, like Fenichel, Reich took seriously the issue that acquisitive pursuits have a strong "rational" component, although his answer to the dilemma sketched above is slightly different.[170] In a discussion of sublimation, Reich notes that irrational and compulsive pursuits begin with a rational element that undergoes a transformation. These "socially rational" pursuits begin with "infantile – instinctual actions serving the rational urge for pleasure." It is the social (familial) repression of the infantile wish which forces it to become irrational in the form of the symbolic satisfaction of an unconscious wish (in this case through the process of sublimation).[171] Reich thought he detected in this back and forth process in the human psyche the same sort of dialectical transformation that Marx called attention to in the historical/economic sphere.[172]

However, the important point, from the perspective of this book, is not how the debate between Fenichel and Reich (as to who is most correct in his interpretation of Marx and Freud) should be resolved; but rather the fact that both authors were limited by their adherence to an orthodox Marxist view which has real difficulties accounting for major changes in a *late stage* capitalist society such as exists today (where, e.g., the economy is highly regulated); most significantly, there is a greater emphasis and proliferation in the area of *consumption* (this issue was addressed earlier, and room does not permit for further elaboration here).[173] An example of such a limitation, from Fenichel's essay, can be found on page 92, where he talks as if it is only the "capitalist" who *"must strive to accumulate wealth."*[174] In our present society, almost all sectors or classes are now subject to such compulsion. As I noted earlier, Reich was criticized by at least one contemporary Marxist for "starting with consumption" rather than "production."[175] However, it turns out that the consumption referred to here, is sexual activity and not consumer products; and, although Reich, as will be seen, had some very interesting things to say about the addiction to work, he failed to address directly the issue of addiction to consumption. This having been said, there are still a number of areas where Reich advances the argument of this book.

Reich's greatest contribution was in the analysis of the formation and nature of character; in particular, how social ideology gets reproduced "in the head." One expert notes that "Reich's psychology emphasized the historical flexibility of the instincts and the social specificity of the frustrations they encounter."[176] The process by which society "reproduces" its economic and political ideology begins, Reich asserts, well before the formation of the superego (out of the parental superego); it begins with "the earliest frustrations and identifications", with the pre-oedipal, beginnings of the formation of character.[177] The agent for this reproductive process, in our society, is the *patriarchal,* nuclear family (here the question of

190

manipulation, addressed above, gets pushed back to an earlier stage of development). Reich's historical and anthropological speculations about the origins of this family structure and its sexual suppression, (based largely on Engels and Bronislaw Malinowski), like Freud's similar ventures, are one of the weakest points in his theory (there are some good feminist critiques of Engels on family origins, as well as reevaluations of Malinowski on the oedipus complex).[178] However, it is not necessary to accept the specifics of Reich's pioneering theory to see that his main point about the socializing influence of different types of family structure is important for this book. Nancy Chodorow's own study of this "reproduction" process begins with Reich's observation that, in our society, during the crucial early years of the formation of character, the mother is the primary socializing agent.[179] The specific mode of repression which the infant experiences "is itself a historically specific act which reflects the individual's internalization of the prevailing mode of social relations."[180] Unlike Freud, Reich did not accept the conflict between the instinctual and the social as an inevitable feature of life, but rather as the outgrowth of the needs of our historically specific authoritarian society.[181] It follows that in a less repressive society the kind of character pathology sketched below would not be found. This contrast between Freud and Reich should not be drawn too sharply, however: once again, things are more complicated, in that Freud held that each generation was forced to uphold the repression handed down by former generations, a view similar to Reich's concept of *tradition.* [182] Also, Reich believed in a basic conservative principle of social change caused by the fact that character, once established, changes much more slowly than social institutions. [183]

Reich's major contribution to an understanding of this process of character formation came in his magnum opus on *Character Analysis.* [184] It was seen earlier in this chapter that Reich's concept of an "armor-plating of character" had a strong influence on Anna Freud's theory of defense mechanisms. Reich postulated what can be seen as a continuum, with flexibility at the healthy end and rigidity at the pathological pole (a parallel continuum could be drawn for the treatment experience, with increasing "character resistance" at the tenacious end). The purpose of this "hardening" process (in which characteristic modes of reacting —or dispositions — become increasingly chronic and automatic) "is to protect the ego from external and internal dangers."[185] The experience of "unpleasure" (*Unlust*),

that is, the frustration of instinctual demands is what leads to the

contraction of the armor around the ego (with pleasurable experiences having

an opening up effect). This process of increased hardening of the ego has three

parts: It identifies with the frustrating reality as personified in the

figure of the main suppressive person. It turns against itself the

aggression which it mobilized against the suppressive person and which

also produced the anxiety. It develops reactive attitudes toward the

sexual strivings, i.e., it utilizes the energy of these strivings to serve its

own purposes, namely to ward them off.[186]

There are a number of conditions (some of them social) which

determine the development of a particular character structure (e.g., the

stage of development and the specific instincts involved in conflict).

These work together with specific defense mechanisms (in particular,

identification, sublimation, and reaction formation) to help resolve the

conflict. The specific way in which conflict is resolved depends upon the

structure of the character. "And *which* instinctual forces are employed to

establish the character and which are allowed direct gratification decides

the difference not only between health and sickness but among the individual character types."[187] The character type, that Reich discusses, which comes closest to the pleonexic is the compulsive character; and, the defense linked closely with the compulsive is reaction formation.[188] In this, he was a pioneer in developing a psychoanalytic understanding of behaviors such as hoarding, seeing it as an adaptive reaction. The idea here seems to be that the "reactive performance", rather than being motivated directly by a desire, comes about when an instinct is blocked, leading to increased restlessness, with growing "irritability and even anxiety."[189]The example that Reich examines is, what would be called today, the 'workaholic', the person for whom "work is an escape from rest." Reich believes that the achievements of this individual are "less successful socially", than in the case of sublimation, because there is a wider gap between latent capabilities and actual achievement; but why this should be is not made clear. In any case, the result is often "feelings of inferiority."[190] Reich maintains that work in our culture is much more often of this compulsive and robotic variety, because of educational and social conditions; but again, he does not spell out why. The reaction formation has the effect of turning the drive against the self; a process he calls "inversion." It is an example of repression, since the original goal

194

remains active, though suppressed, in the worker's unconscious. For this

reason, the reaction formation continues to have its effect, and has a

tendency to spread throughout the personality.[191] The compulsive activity,

thereby, takes on other defensive qualities, such as denial and rationalization.

A "symptom neurosis" can result because the unconscious sexual and

aggressive drive has been "damned up" (a clear example of Freud's libido

theory or hydraulic model). In a later section of the book, Reich outlines the

well-known traits of the compulsive character which derive from anal

eroticism (among others, he mentions in passing: "inability to husband

money" and a "strong passion for *collecting* things").[192] However, he adds

nothing to explain why fixation on this particular erotic stage of

development should lead to formation of these specific dispositions, other

than the now familiar and unhelpful arguments of too-early toilet training and

the symbolic equation of feces with money. Nor is the argument advanced,

when it is learned later that other forms of addictive behavior ("especially

alcoholism") results from a fixation at the "phallic-narcissistic stage", a

protection from "regression to the passive and anal stages" (as will be seen in

a moment, this same behavior was attributed by Abraham to a

fixation at the *oral* stage). Reich's greatest contribution remains his recognition of the social and political determinants of compulsive dispositions. In a later work, he summarizes these main influencing factors which are added to the biological.[193] They include a "fear of freedom" which adds to characterological rigidity (in effect fear of flexibility), as well as an interest in money and power as a substitute for unfulfilled happiness in love. Before concluding this chapter with an analysis of how some contemporary psychoanalysts have built upon these insights, the contribution of one final contemporary of Freud — Karl Abraham — needs to be briefly examined.

In a number of his papers, most specifically his short essay on "The Spending of Money in Anxiety States," Abraham implicitly raises an issue of central concern to this book, namely, how pleonexia can be differentiated from several related inclinations (the principle topic of the fourth and concluding chapter below).[194] Abraham begins his essay on "Spending" by inadvertently calling attention to a logical dilemma in the psychoanalytic literature on character traits: namely, the fact that the same causal or etiological factor (i.e., fixation at the anal stage of development) is invoked to explain what are very opposite types of behavior. Abraham notes that much had been written about the anal character traits of "neurotic avarice and the anxious retention

of money," but in his experience there exists *another* group of neurotics who

display the very opposite behavior of impulsive spending (a symptom

which comes over them "like a kind of attack"). In a later essay he

complicates things further by stating that it is the *same* group of neurotics

which engages in both retention and liberal spending.[195] Although

Abraham retains the explanation in terms of anal eroticism, he

provides some additional explanations for this specific type of

compulsive behavior based on his experience with three clinical cases.

Before looking at these additional factors, a word needs to be said by way of

possible clarification concerning this dilemma.

One possible rejoinder might be that there is a more general

character structure or disposition to behave in certain ways under certain

circumstances, and what is being observed here is simply the variations in

behavior caused by variations in circumstances. But this is clearly not

what is being argued in these essays or elsewhere; and too general a

character structure would prove quite vacuous when it came to

explaining specific behaviors. Another possibility is that this is an example

of the "mixed products of two different sources of character-formation" that Abraham notes in an essay on "Oral Eroticism and Character."[196] But, although this explanation would at least work, it is clearly not what Abraham has in mind when talking of anal eroticism. Perhaps the best defense would be to borrow Freud's notion of the different components of an instinct, and to say that what is being observed in these cases is the displacement of associated ideas or symptoms on to different objects. The overall problem of the differentiation of a specific set of behaviors or syndrome will come up again in analyzing Abraham's important essay on "Manic-Depressive States and Obsessional Neurosis", where he states that "the same abnormalities of behavior in relation to money and possessions" exist in both the "melancholic character and the obsessional neurotic."[197]

No matter how this methodological issue is resolved, Abraham makes a number of interesting observations and suggestions concerning the compulsive spender. The major additional factor which he postulates is, what would be called today (following Margaret Mahler), an infantile problem with separation-individuation from the parental home. In terms of Freudian economics: "leaving the home signifies to the unconscious a detachment of the libido from its object."[198]This process of separation creates the anxiety states, and the defensive reaction is to spend money as if it were libido.

In terms of Reich's theory: a false internal perception of ego flexibility is created in what remains a very rigid character structure. The end result is a quite temporary relief of anxiety which is soon replaced by a new flood (no doubt accompanied by added guilt over the expenditure). Abraham makes a couple of additional interesting observations in this densely packed essay: (1) he notes that his patients engage in certain rationalizations of their behavior (what he calls elsewhere, in an essay on alcoholics, "cover-motives"; (2) he, also, remarks on how one patient admitted to frequently intensifying her anxiety in order to have an excuse to spend (an addictive setup, also, frequently observed in alcoholics); (3) finally, he makes the very important observation that this form of compulsive behavior often acts as a "substitute gratification" for the love which their rigid character prevents them from giving and receiving.[199] This latter factor is particularly strong in those individuals who buy and accumulate possessions in order to give them away (in the hopes of receiving love in return — a feature that can be seen in kleptomania also); as well as those who strive for money and commodities because they believe it enhances their sexual appeal (a fact not lost on the advertising industry, as I noted earlier in this book). Abraham elaborates on this connection between addiction and erotic longing in his essay on "Sexuality and Alcoholism."[200] In this early study, Abraham speaks more frequently of the social factors which contribute to the development and continuation of this disorder. In particular, the cultural link between the idea of manliness and consumption of large amounts of alcohol. In addition, the important connection between intoxication and sexual excitement could be applied equally well to the addictive rush This is what Michael Schneider calls "commodity euphoria," the "narcotizing atmosphere ... which is a slightly psychotic condition where the ego denies a part of reality so as to surrender itself to the hallucinatory wish" that comes with the acquisition of commodities by the pleonexic. Schneider notes that it is only within "the ritual of buying that the commodity has this narcotic effect."[201]

Finally, in his pioneering study of "Oral Eroticism and Character" Abraham takes up again the issue of an "inordinate desire to possess" in an effort to differentiate between those disorders which stem from anal characteristics and those which come from a fixation or regression to the oral stage.[202] He notes that for largely social reasons more of the oral component is allowed to continue in "normal" (i.e., "genital") sexual life (this has probably not been true in all cultures or periods of history, e.g., the ancient Greek). Most importantly, he notes that abnormal parsimony and avarice have a close relation to an early oral or sucking component, which later gets transferred to the anal sphincter. And he appears, at first, to make the interesting observation that such behaviors can have a purely social cause, totally independent of "the anal sources of character-formation."[203] However, when he notes that these disorders are "often met within people who are inhibited from properly earning a livelihood", he is not referring to the social effects of poverty on money disorders, but rather the effects of disappointment of oral desires in the early years, which leave these individuals with extreme anxiety lest they lose what they do possess. However, this observation on the early effects of deprivation *could* in fact, be generalized to the hypothesis that it leads to greater craving for possessions in adult life.

Michael Schneider (following the psychoanalyst R. Reiche) makes some interesting suggestions about the relationship between anal and oral characteristics in the pleonexic.[204] Reiche had noted that

201

the late stage capitalist need for increased consumption meant that the rigid and parsimonious features of the anal-compulsive character needed to be "loosened up." In other words, the old oral character traits, which Abraham noted are the foundation on which the anal traits are built, needed to be "hauled out of their repressed state," so that the consumer could learn to respond to the "sensuous appeal" of commodities; (this is the process which Campbell called the "new hedonism").[205] The late stage capitalist consumer, therefore, is subject to "oral-addictive" characteristics (in response to the process in which, as Wilhelm Reich observed, a society creates the character structures it needs). Of course, it can always be argued that, since the "experience of satisfaction" is an oral experience, then, (as Laplanche & Pontalis, note) "desire and satisfaction are forever marked by this first experience."[206] In any case, this hypothesis of Schneider/Reiche, has the decided advantage of showing the many connections between pleonexia and the so-called oral-addictive disorders, such as alcoholism.

Some of these connections are noted briefly in a paper on "Some Emotional Uses of Money" by William Kaufman.[207] In a small section on "Compulsive Spending," Kaufman notes how the compulsive spender becomes increasingly anxious if "he is not able to immediately satisfy his slightest desire for spending" and will often go into debt rather than forego this satisfaction.[208] Kaufman further notes that one unconscious motivation for "getting rid" of one's money, can be a desire "to return to a passive-dependent status as a result of self-inflicted poverty."[209]Kaufman asserts that, "the history of many of these compulsive spenders indicates that they were overprotected in their early childhood by an overindulgent parent who guiltily substituted liberal money gifts for love and affection. Usually one parent was strict, but the other one overcompensated for his severity."[210]

Kaufman further notes that spending his parent's money at an alarming rate can be, in such cases, a way of punishing them for withholding their true affection. Spending on themselves in adulthood can become "an unconsciously overdetermined means of giving themselves something akin to love."[211] Kaufman notes also that some compulsive spenders engage in deprivations followed by spending binges, "enjoying the intense sensual pleasure of being able to buy anything he wants" (a process obviously akin to other addictions). Another group will engage in various antisocial activities in order to have this sensual pleasure (examples include: passing worthless checks, prostitution, and, of course, gambling). Finally, Kaufman calls attention to those individuals who spend compulsively during periods of depression; as a form of self-medication one might add. Kaufman's list of compulsive spending behaviors raises, once again, the issue of delineation of a specific syndrome of pleonexia (i.e., whether what is being enumerated is simply a list of unrelated symptoms from different disorders, with the only common feature being the use of commodities to achieve one's end). Despite the fact that the same objection could be directed against any other addiction, it will be taken seriously and addressed in the concluding chapter. However, before turning directly to that project, a few brief remarks about contemporary psychoanalytic contributions will prove helpful.

It was noted at the beginning of this chapter that there has been virtual silence about the topic of this book from contemporary psychoanalysts. A similar silence can be seen in the feminist literature, despite strong anecdotal evidence that women suffer more from pleonexia (two women who talk around the subject are Christine Delphy, 1984 and Nancy Hartsock, 1983). Therefore, only a few suggestive observations from the psychoanalytic literature on addiction need be noted here before turning to the two exceptions — David Krueger and Joel Kovel (Kovel's remarks are unsystematic and sketchy, though important).

In a textbook on the topic of *Psychoanalysis of Drug Dependence,* J. Winstead Adams (1978) provides a very brief survey of much of the relevant literature under the general heading of narcissism; the principle assertion being that drug addiction is simply a symptom of this more general preoedipal (pregenital) disorder.[212] A more recent and more systematic study, one which recognizes the existence of specific addiction syndromes, will serve here as an example of this contemporary approach. Chelton & Bonney give a definition of addiction that emphasizes compulsive behavioral patterns despite their harmful effects to all aspects of life.[213] A wide number of habitual behaviors used, not only to regulate emotions, but also to "help maintain order and continuity in the sense of self (aliveness, vigor, psychic cohesion, and calmness)."[214] Among such behaviors the authors include "excessive spending."[215] In their analysis of these harmful behaviors, the authors utilize the tools and categories of two psychoanalysts in particular — Heinz Kohut and D.W. Winnicott. The primary understanding is that the addictions represent a failure in self-cohesion and self-development caused by regression; in less technical terms, an attempt to counter feelings of emptiness and personal isolation. Such internal functions as regulation of feelings, self-esteem, and maintenance of ideals and goals, as well as non-harmful techniques of self-soothing are what are specifically lacking in these individuals. A number of different psychic strategies are used in a futile attempt to fill the inner void; including, "intellectualization, forced thinking, obsessive ritualistic behavior, and the creating of real or fantasized risk taking or crises."[216] Cross addiction is a frequent observation; and, the authors note that eating disorders are commonly seen with excessive spending.

When it comes to the question of etiology these authors take strong issue with the drive theorists who have been the major focus of earlier pages of this chapter. Their critique of these early biological models represents an important advance in understanding. For these critical psychoanalysts, the compulsive force behind the addictions is the more global need for interpersonal relations — "a pull instead of a push."[217].

206

The type of drives represented by anal and oral needs are simply "fragmentation products" of this more general need, the results of inevitable "self object empathic failures." The terminology and concepts are borrowed from Kohut, an author whose ideas seem closest to the concerns raised by William Leiss,, in particular the problem of fragmentation of self and needs created by commodities (Kohut will be examined indirectly through his influence on Kovel, an influence which was not uncritical). Chelton and Bonney also make an interesting use of Winnicott's famous concept of the transitional object one which seems to fit the pleonexic best of all. They note that the transitional object plays an important role in the separation-individuation process by serving as "an inanimate substitute maternal self object."[218] During a healthy development the child should move beyond transitional objects by developing personal autonomy or "self-regulating " ego by internalizing idealized empathic relationships outside her immediate family.[219] Chelton and Bonney suggest that if this step in healthy development is less than adequate for whatever reason the result can be that "the use of the transitional object may be excessively prolonged and take on the characteristics of an addiction."[220]. In other words, the transitional object is maintained in order to provide the kind of psychic needs and feeling states alluded to earlier in their essay. It can be argued that the role of commodities and addictive collecting fits this mechanism best of all. It was seen earlier in the analysis of Fenichel that self-esteem and personal identity are pronounced problems, and both Abraham and Kaufman noted how separation- individuation problems are particularly pronounced in pleonexics. Finally, many examples of isolation from interpersonal contact can be found in pleonexics. I have known of one example where a client spent many years of his life hiding in his apartment, fearful to answer the door or the telephone because of his many creditors. Incidentally, in my experience, the devastating effects of such behavior patterns on family members is another way in which this addiction is like most others. This is another way in which hoarding behaviors lead to isolation and family problems. Chilton and Bonney conclude from this, as well as from their own clinical experience, that peer-support groups are the most effective treatment approach with such addictive disorders (more on the topic of treatment below).

Before leaving this topic of the relationship of narcissism and addiction, another author who advances understanding of consumer pathologies needs to be briefly mentioned. Arnold Rothstein's book on *The Narcissistic Pursuit of Perfection* emphasizes the powerful role which man's delusional pursuit of perfection plays in narcissistic disorders, a process which can be itself an "addictive pursuit."[221]. The first thing to note is that Rothstein sees narcissism as a structural disorder in "the basic core of dispositions and trends" which make up an individual's character; and, as such, the behaviors involved are "chronic." What becomes distorted in these patients is the "ubiquitous potential" for "pursuit of illusions of narcissistic perfection."[222] Rothstein follows Kohut in seeing the addictions as one part of a subcategory of this characterological problem, which Kohut labeled "narcissistic behavior disorders" (the other category is "narcissistic personality disorders"). This former category of patients is, in contrast to the latter group, capable of forming transference relations due to an inclination toward sadistic behavior. Kohut, therefore, calls the addictions "alloplastic" (borrowing this term from Ferenczi, 1930).[223] Alloplastic behaviors are those where the libido turns away from self toward external objects or persons. In an earlier work, Kohut had borrowed another label for such behaviors, calling them "other-directed."[224]

209

Although such relational behavior might appear to be an expression of health, they are actually dependent cravings based on pathologically damaged superegos (for this reason Kohut places them alongside other antisocial behaviors). In fact, Kohut maintained that drugs do not result from the absence of loving relationships, "but as a replacement for a defect in the psychological structure"— a view which would appear to be hard to reconcile with the position held by Chelton & Bonney.[225] In any case, the important contrast with early drive theorists is Kohut's assertion that it is need for relationships (rather than 'objects' in the usual sense of this word) that is the motivating force behind addictive behavior.[226]

These views of Kohut on addictions also had a substantial influence on the last two psychoanalysts who will be examined in this book (the only contemporary analysts with a major interest in pleonexia), namely, Joel Kovel and David Krueger. Kovel's major work, *The Age of Desire* (1981) is a sophisticated blend of biography, case studies, fiction, and theory, written from a critical and politically radical perspective. The issues of most relevance to this book are not systematically examined; and, therefore, observations need to be pulled from different parts of his work. Although he was clearly influenced by

Kohut and Lacan (among others), his is a maverick work, not beholden to any orthodoxy whether of the right or left. If there is an overall perspective, it is always to remain aware of the dialectical play of complex social, political and psychological forces (which include the activity and personality of the analyst), that go into the creation and maintenance of any behavioral disorder. For this reason Kovel's approach lends itself well to examination of a pathological condition with the complexity of influencing factors that go into the makeup of pleonexia. Among his principle concerns is the "split between historical role and personal characteristics," a split that Alasdair MacIntyre recognized as one of the primary causes of modern disorders and disaffections.[227] Kovel always tries to remain aware of the role which power and domination play in creating and maintaining our social and psychiatric problems. Both Kovel and MacIntyre see the great theoretical need for "a notion of human potentiality, what men and women could be, given the overcoming of historical domination."[228] For Kovel, the great value of psychoanalysis as a tool to achieve this goal is its contextual, historical, and holistic approach.[229] The one element, in Freud, that retards progress is his "dualism" between the physical and the cultural. Kovel contrasts

211

this with a view he calls "dialectical," one in which individuals interact and "transform" their environment.[230] Psychoanalysis, nonetheless, recognizes "transhistorical" factors in human nature, such as "desire", and it is the "discourse" of these elements which analysts seek to illuminate. This analysis of desire needs to be modified in light of recent discoveries about infant psychology, but the reality of a "prolonged dependency," still applies.[231] Finally, the transhistorical element which sets us apart is our basically social nature, what Marx referred to when he called the "self" an "ensemble of social relations." Like Reich, Kovel believes that there is no transhistorical need, however, for desire to become problematic, rather it is the culture of capitalism which necessitates the alienation and splitting which are observed in the pathologies of self (whether this basically optimistic view is accurate or not is really an empirical issue, but can dissolve into a futile nature vs. nurture debate). Like Rothstein, Kovel sees the transhistorical factor in desire that comes from the universal, narcissistic pursuit of perfection; and it is this aspect of desire which the cultural forces of capitalism use for their own ends.[232] Note that narcissism itself, therefore, is not *created* by social forces. Rather, the very nature of desire is that it "tends to flow away from the object and toward the subject, that is, it tends to become *narcissistic*. The object becomes the Other, which collapses back into the self."[233] Desire is on the boundary between the mental and the physical. On the one hand, are the instincts which represent the *"configuration of desire"*; on the other is "the historically arranged disposition of the object world." The interaction between these forces (which Freud termed the "source" and the "aim", as noted above) is "instinctual gratification [which] is not only imaginary, it is historical as well."[234] The similarity to views of Baudrillard, sketched above, is not surprising given the common influence of Lacan. Like William Leiss, Kovel holds that consumer society contributes to a fragmentation of desire.[235] Kovel's case studies all involve examples of such alienation, splitting or fragmentation of desire and self through the process of addictive production and consumption of commodities (although he does not describe a pure case of pleonexia). Each represents a case of self-estrangement or alienation from others; and their analysis illustrates the blending of transhistorical and historical factors. Many of the cultural forces that Kovel sees active in these cases were similar to my analysis above, and do not need to be reexamined here (for instance, the role of advertising in nourishing imagination; its need to keep consumption ongoing; as well as the increasing fragmentation

of self caused in part by proliferation of ever new and quickly obsolete

objects). Kovel's contribution is not only to put these concepts into

the terms of contemporary psychoanalysis, but to show how

difficult it is in our society to carry on interpersonal relations which go

beyond the purely instrumental interactions promoted by

consumption (i.e., to treat others as ends rather than as means).

And it is ultimately in the treatment process that the patient is asked

to learn, not only what are the factors that block intimacy, but how to

begin to practice intimacy as well. Kovel's suggestions for an

expanded treatment process will be examined further at the end of

this book.

David Krueger (1988) is the only contemporary

psychoanalyst to examine pleonexia in a systematic way. As noted

above, his approach to this problem is from a self psychology perspective.

His general conclusion is "that compulsive shopping represents an

attempt at affect regulation, especially to remedy depression and

emptiness and is a chronic pattern."[236]Krueger sees 'pleonexia' (his

term is compulsive shopping and spending) as a distinct disorder and, therefore, to be distinguished from a number of other symptom patterns which revolve around the use of money. Krueger notes that the patients with pleonexia with whom he has had contact seem to have certain characteristics in common: (1) first, they have all been women (something which he notes only in passing; see below for a critique of this omission); (2) the developmental deficit common to this group "involves a developmental arrest of the body self as well as the psychological self"; (3) all but one of his patients suffers from bulimia; (4) the onset of the disorder is usually in early adolescence; (5) parenting usually involves the substitution of material objects for needed emotional connectedness; (6) and, the compulsion to shop involves a doomed effort to find the empathy missing from childhood or other human relationships in the objects acquired.[237] Krueger's main contention is that the pleonexic is driven by certain features of narcissistic character pathology: specifically, these women suffer from an inner emptiness and lack of "stable self-image." This lack manifests itself in an over concern with personal appearance and all aspects of "body ego." Most of their shopping binges involve the purchase of clothing or other items for enhancing body self and image. These binges usually occur during periods of depression brought on by problems with significant relationships or from other narcissistic injury; and represent, Krueger argues, a feeble attempt at self-soothing. This connection of pleonexia with body image and clothing has been remarked on earlier in this chapter (particularly, in the discussion of Fenichel; note, also, that Chilton & Bonney discuss attempts at self-soothing and cross addiction to eating disorders). Krueger's brief analysis, in fact, brings together a number of key points made earlier in this chapter, and will prove very useful in the effort to further differentiate these disorders. The absence of even a passing reference to gender or cultural issues in this regard is particularly glowing in Krueger's article (for more on this issue see below).

In his insightful and beautifully written paper, "To hold on or to let go? Loss and substitution in the process of hoarding," the Irish analyst John O'Connor (2014) shows how a psychodynamic approach can provide a rich understanding of the causal factors behind hoarding. O'Connor draws on years of psychoanalytic research on our normal difficulties with mourning, transience, and loss, and with the very human reluctance to let go, in order to shed light on the psychic processes involved in hoarding disorder. O'Connor shows how recent research findings about individuals with hoarding problems dovetail nicely with these psychoanalytic insights. Three discoveries are of special relevance: (1) the intense fear of losing things that is so prominent in hoarding; (2) a strong correlation between the onset of hoarding and traumatic loss; and, evidence that individuals who hoard have a tendency to relate more strongly to objects than to people.[238] These findings dovetail with the research, discussed in the chapter on cultural influences above, demonstrating that individuals with pleonexia or materialist values score low on social intimacy scales. Also, O'Connor's hypothesis that hoarding involves a defensive reaction to "unresolved and unprocessed loss," resonates most strongly with the many cases of hoarding in seniors, so-called "late-life hoarding."

In his conclusion, O'Connor gestures toward the many other types of consumer pathology that can benefit, as this chapter has shown, from the many insights into deep human emotions that have come from the long history of psychoanalytic research.

Conclusion

The real measure of security is not what you have, but
what you can do without.
Joseph Wood Krutch

You must bind me hard and fast, so that I cannot stir
from the spot where you will stand me … and if I beg
you to release me, you must tighten and add to my
bonds.
Homer, *The Odyssey*

Whoever has the most stuff when he dies, wins.
Anonymous

Krishnamurti's comment, at the beginning of this book,
about conformity to a sick society is not health, should remind us
that a positive outcome of psychotherapy may not simply be to get
the client/patient to conform to society's norms for good behavior.
Nor should the therapist be in the business of choosing which
social roles a particular client finds most fulfilling or life-
affirming, whether it be grandmother, teacher, or entrepreneur.

However, the therapist should help the individual determine which set of behaviors or dispositions contribute to achieving his or her goals, and which are leading to pain and suffering. Borrowing from Alasdair MacIntyre, we have seen that a central feature of therapy should be to help the client determine which set of behaviors are internal to the social roles she values, and which behaviors lead to external goods. It is interesting to note that this understanding of the goals of psychotherapy has significant features in common with the positive clinical psychology approach, such as the importance of building strengths of character, and the role of institutions and therapy in enabling or hindering these internal virtues.[1]

The question of personal freedom of action has been central (though not always center stage) in this book. In chapter 2, it was a question of possible *external coercion* — manufactured desire or, what was labeled *the manipulationist thesis.* In chapter 3, the issue of *internal* compulsion was seen to be Freud's revolutionary contribution to a new (and much more complex) theory of action and desire. Unconscious intentional states (impulses, desires, cognitions, or motives) came into conflict with internalized norms in the form of the superego; and they are, therefore, repressed. But, nevertheless, they continue somehow to exert a repetitive, compulsive or pressing force on behavior. This force leads to anxiety and, ultimately, the construction of compromise intentional states which are symbolically associated with the original states.

Psychoanalysis was, therefore, from its very beginnings concerned with the existence of internal conflict and coercion; and the goal of therapy was to "replace compulsive and uncontrolled behavior by voluntary and deliberate conduct."[2] Freud, like Hegel and Schopenhauer before him, was a proponent of the futility of desire. But, unlike his predecessors, Freud saw the instability and compulsive nature of desire as an innate and biological process of the organism.[3] Therefore, the external or social coercive forces play a subordinate role in his drama.

The principle contention of this book, however, is that both types of influencing forces, the internal as well as the external are required to reinforce each other in order to produce an ongoing disposition to perform compulsive behaviors such as compulsive buying, spending, and hoarding. For certain desires to take on a compulsive form, not only must the true source of the desire be unconsciously repressed, but the object and aim of the associated or compromise desire must be socially reinforced. Furthermore, for the behavior to become painful or otherwise problematic for the individual, it needs to result in social and/or physiologically negative consequences. This is a major reason why a disorder like hoarding can be so difficult to treat. Clinical treatment needs to take into consideration such social and cultural factors in order to provide a complete theoretical explanation for the central characteristics of these behavioral disorders, especially the lack of awareness and ambivalence that are such a prevalent and frustrating feature for all involved in treatment.

It is because of these biopsychosocial components that the treatment of these disorders, especially hoarding disorder, ideally should involve a multidisciplinary, management team approach, with a focus on psychoeducation (including for family), peer support, neurological and cognitive assessment, individual and group therapy, and concrete problem-solving by legal, housing, and other community workers. Although this may seem overwhelming, the fact is that quite a number of communities have developed a hoarding task force, in the realization that the team approach is the only way to address the poor insight and strong denial, as well as the complex social issues involved with hoarding. Many of these same tools, such as credit counseling services, will be needed for full recovery from spending and acquiring disorders. A society that has done so much to promote pleonexia has a moral duty to help those most vulnerable to its problems.

Recent research on personality and social psychology has largely confirmed the presence of a defense or coping mechanism of denial, as well as a number of related mechanisms that may be major factors in the very poor insight seen in most individuals with hoarding disorder (other factors, such as cognitive deficits, have been touched on above). Freud's great contribution to an understanding of this ambiguity was to show that, not only are there often unforeseen consequences to what a person intends by her voluntary actions, either as the aim of her ends or those actions she aims at as means to her ends; but also there are situations where an individual intends a particular act, but yet is acting under a compulsion to perform it since it is a "derivative desire" of a forbidden impulse.[4] Pleonexia can be seen as just such a case where coercion and desire reinforce each other. What may have started as a socially sanctioned attempt at self-soothing has taken on a life of its own. A hedonically complex attempt to deal with emotional conflict has itself become problematic, leading to further conflict. The consequences of the compulsion to buy, (e.g., very large debt, feelings of guilt or disappointment, etc) leads to feelings of being out-of-control, helpless, which in turn can bring greater emotional conflict (e.g., low self-esteem, depression, etc). But before this argument can be totally clear, it will be useful to define how pleonexia is different from other similar disorders.

Back in the 1980s, when I first examined the psychological problems in this book, there were only a few studies examining the negative outcomes of consumer behavior.[5] On the other hand, there were literally thousands of studies published that appeared to have been written with the hopes of assisting manufacturers in their efforts to increase demand for their products. I took this to be another indication of the cultural forces nourishing the development and continuance of pleonexia. I did recognize that another explanation could be the possibly small number of psychiatric patients who presented with pleonexia as their *primary* complaint. I reasoned that perhaps such small numbers of patients was itself a reflection of the social sanctioning of compulsive buying and hoarding behavior in our society. I saw the silence about consumer problems as an example of Freud's suggestion that money topics would become a social taboo. Today, it is a credit to the scientific integrity of the academic marketing field that they have followed their data, and taken the lead in writing about the pathological results of our consumer culture.[6] A number of the suggestions for further research that I put forward in 1989 have been conducted, and great deal of useful information is now available. It is also very apparent that problems related to consumer behavior are now endemic in all, so-called, advanced societies. Much to their credit, experts in marketing have acknowledged their social responsibility to the estimated 18 million Americans with compulsive buying problems.[7] It is still very much the case that a great deal of supporting evidence about the proper treatment of consumer disorders can be learned from similar culturally enhanced mental health problem behaviors, such as eating disorders, as well as other impulse control disorders. In 1989, I borrowed on the pioneering work on eating disorders by Stanley Schachter (1971), and Hilde Bruch (1973), the excellent feminist approach of Susan Bordo (1985/86), and the multidimensional approach to anorexia nervosa of Paul Garfinkel, David Garner, and Brunner Mazel (1982). Although I argued for the need to have a broad conception of personal well-being when considering consumer behavior, I also argued for the heuristic value of having a medical illness model. In presenting diagnostic criteria for compulsive buying, I followed the categories of the then current *Diagnostic and Statistical Manuel of Mental*

Disorders (1987, 3rd. revised edition); noting some problems with this approach to classification for personality disorders, as argued by Otto Kernberg.[8]

Although I argued that there were definite features of a personality disorder, in what I called pleonexia, it was the category of "Impulse Control Disorders" that best fit the symptoms of compulsive buying. This category is no longer covered separately, but at the time, there were five specific disorders listed under it: Intermittent Explosive Disorder, Kleptomania, Pathological Gambling, Pyromania, and Trichotillomania (hair-pulling disorder). As I saw it then, pleonexia had the following essential features: a chronic failure to resist urges or desires to buy or to acquire material objects or commodities in other ways; a behavior that compromises, disrupts, or damages personal, family, or vocational pursuits. I argued that pleonexia was a "dispositional disorder," as defined by   Stanley Peele, or a "life style trait," in that it is long-lasting and shows a slow progression.[9] I added, however, that the behavior most often occurs in a pattern of impulsive episodes or "shopping binges."[10] In an early reference to hoarding disorder, I noted that objects are often accumulated to a quantity well beyond their usefulness, frequently creating substantial problems of storage. The example I gave, borrowed from Craig MacAndrew, was of one individual who was injured in an earthquake by the 9,900 books in his 12 foot square hotel apartment room.[11] I noted the same feelings of shame and guilt that come from compulsive buying, when an individual spends more

224

than he can afford, thereby neglecting the needs of his children. As with substance addiction, there is a growing preoccupation with acquiring, as well as an extensive fantasy life revolving around the ownership of commodities.[12] I noted that this preoccupation, as well as the urge or impulse to acquire, and the actual behavior, all increase substantially during periods of disturbed mood, especially feelings of depression, depletion, or inner emptiness and tension. Another similar feature of compulsive buying and the addictions, that I noted, was the positive feelings of excitement or euphoria (a high), but also the feelings of anxiousness, helplessness, guilt, and even panic that often accompanies acquisitive behavior.[13] I added that there was often restlessness and irritability if the behavior continued.

Many studies from the 1970s and 1980s noted associated problems with compulsive acquisition, such as defaulting on debts or other financial responsibilities, difficulties coping with rising levels of financial debt, resulting in disrupted personal relationships, increased disapproval from significant others, a number of antisocial behaviors (including shoplisting, borrowing from illegal sources, forgery, embezzlement, fraud, and tax evasion — I noted that any criminal behavior was usually nonviolent). It is important to note that all of these negative consequences have only increased in frequency and severity in subsequent decades. The early case studies already pointed to findings about the strong correlation between individuals with materialist values, such as personal appearance, and external

225

approval, resulting from a lack of the kind of ego strengths so important to positive psychologists today. As early as 1988, David Krueger called attention to the strong relationship between traumatic loss and compulsive buying, an important feature now associated with hoarding disorder, as I noted above. Ruth Formenek had already offered independent evidence that, especially for women who are beyond middle age in our society, "involvement with things may compensate for the loss of people, role, and status."[14]

I have argued throughout this book that, in light of these multiple problems, as well as the strong social and cultural influences, only a multidisciplinary, team approach to treatment can be truly effective with pathological consumer behavior. It should also be clear that long term group therapy needs to be a major component of any treatment strategy. It is not coincidental that the movement to force short term psychotherapy coincided with major transformations in our political economy, including the gradual mutation and imposition of a consumer value system on every discipline, even fields such as sports, medicine, and social work that have had very different primary values. The irony of this transformation, as it effects those individuals who suffer from problematic consumer behavior, is palpable.

I also noted, back in 1989, that individuals who suffer from consumer pathologies tend to have very poor insight regarding the true cause of their suffering, and that they, therefore, usually present, if at all, with other complaints, such as anxiety or

226

depression. I noted that this aspect of these disorders should not be surprising in light of the culturally-syntonic aspect of behaviors related to their onset.

The fact that our political system is becoming more addictive to gambling as a source of funding will inevitably lead to an increase in gambling addiction as a "co-morbid condition," closely associated with attempts to try and relieve spending problems. The strong evidence for an early onset for all these disorders means that a society that values the flourishing and good mental health of its citizens should invest in early detection and prevention. Given the high prevalence of legal difficulties, especially with hoarding disorder and housing, society has an obligation to provide resources for legal assistance, as well as credit counseling services to sufferers of these disorders.

Differential Diagnosis

The strong role that status and image play in disorders of acquisition helps to explain the predisposing factor of personality disorders, especially Narcissistic Personality Disorder. A great deal has been written about this since I and others first drew attention to the association back in the late 1980s.[15] These narcissistic features have been enumerated above, and do not need to be addressed here, except to point out that they contribute greatly to denial and to intensity of treatment. One narcissistic feature that I addressed in my early study was the displacement of self-image on to materialistic possessions, and this needs to be generalized beyond the emphasis on women and body image, and clothing. It is certainly still the case that there are strong social and political forces effecting women's body image that contribute to some compulsive buying. Also, the more subtle relationship between the sense of power that women describe when shopping can still play a role in developing this disorder. I called attention to the fact that there are important gender issues in the way that feelings of power, even grandiosity, get displaced onto material possessions, noting that these differences were largely ignored by the authors in Morrison (1986; I referred to the good summary of the social and political forces affecting women's body image in Mintz, 1986 and Barthel, 1988). I, also, noted that, at least the strength of such feelings of personal enhancement and power, is directly relatable to the limitations on personal expression placed on women in a patriarchal society. Annie Reich called attention to the male counterpart of expressing power through their cars (1986, p.52). Reich had also called attention to evidence that "overstrong body narcissism is rooted in traumatic experience," and I noted that there was similar evidence of a connection between pleonexia and a history of such trauma.

Psychologists Jean Twenge and Keith Campbell, in their popular 2009 book, *The Narcissism Epidemic* provide a lot of updated evidence for this connection between narcissism, materialism, and consumer pathology. Although they take issue with one contribution of psychodynamic theory, namely the view

228

that narcissism "masks" insecurity and feelings of low self-worth, they make good use of other discoveries by Freud and his followers (pp.24–28; for the record, in my own experience of almost fifty years, I encountered many examples of individuals confirming this "mask model"). Although Twenge and Campbell have important things to say about narcissistic personality disorder, their primary concern is to document the epidemic of, so-called "normal" individuals, with some narcissistic traits, as well as the social and cultural changes that have contributed to this pervasive part of American culture. Others, for example Baudrillard, have referred to the narcissistic character of our consumer society.[16] However, though they never use the term pleonexia, many of the behaviors Twenge and Campbell describe, especially wanting and using more than ones fair share, fit perfectly with the disposition I have described in this book. One relating factor between pathological consumer behavior and someone with narcissistic traits is the obvious fact that "it is harder to show off not having stuff" (p.177). Twenge and Campbel note that the expense of renting public storage units, in order to hold on to more stuff is, largely, an American phenomenon that surprises people from other countries. They carefully document the many social, economic, and environmental problems that have resulted from our consumer behavior, as well as the strong evidence, noted earlier in this book, that materialism leads to deficits in well-being, over a long perspective. They are careful to give both sides and to offer solutions for change, including child-rearing, education, and with the media.

I have noted the relationship between narcissism and perfectionism, both in my early writing on pleonexia, and, especially, in my description of hoarding disorder above. It was Freud who first described "narcissistic perfectionism" in connection with the development of an ego ideal.[17] Once again, it is in the area of personal beauty and strength that this pursuit of perfection contributes to the addictive quality of pleonexia. Annie Reich describes how "self-conscious" and "exhibitionistic" tendencies arising out of feelings of inadequacy can often take the form of acquiring garments, cars, and other commodities.[18] The use of material objects by parents as a substitute for affection, noted above, but also by Twenge and Campbell in their chapter on child-rearing, was, arguably, first addressed by Karen Horney as an important factor in the craving for commodities.[19] She noted that it can lead to an identification of the idealized parent imago with material possessions. Krueger's cases of compulsive buyers offer an illustration of how these "primitive attempts to stimulate a body self-expression and representation" can lead to problematic behavior.

Another psychodynamic feature, which I described in connection with Abraham and Kaufman in the previous chapter, is the existence of anxieties relating from problems with the separation-individuation process. Kaufman, in particular, noticed that the kind of parental substitution of objects for affection, alluded to above, can lead to a desire to regress to what he calls "a passive-dependent status as a result of self-inflicted poverty" resulting from anxieties of separation.[20] The importance of this mechanism in the development of narcissistic personality disorder has been commented on by many authors.[21] Bursten's subtype of this disorder, which is the one most similar to pleonexia, is, also, the type where he finds such separation-individuation problems to be most prominent. The evidence is very strong that, at least in part, compulsive buying behavior is an effort to deal, however unsuccessfully, with such separation anxiety.

The final psychodynamic feature common to the narcissistic personality and the pleonexic is the pathological expression of certain introjects. The process of introjections was intimately connected with the pleasure-ego and oral incorporation for Freud; and, it is not surprising, therefore, to see it connected as well with pleonexia.[22] Meissner describes two correlative forms of introject common in the narcissistic personality, that he calls the "superior-introject" and the "inferior-introject."[23] Behind feelings of shame and worthlessness, Meissner argues, one can find entitlement and grandiosity. Twenge and Campbel may be correct that many individuals with only "normal" narcissistic traits do not suffer from such feelings; but, as Abraham also noted, full mental disorders, such as depression and bipolar disorder often involve feelings of self-reproach and lack of self-regard emanating from the introjected lost love-object caused by the use of material objects.[24] Krueger's case histories of compulsive buyers show

231

several examples of where binge spending is brought on by feelings of depression following the traumatic breakup of a love relationship.

Before leaving the topic of the relationship between pleonexia and narcissistic personality traits, it will be useful to ask the question: which of the four subcategories of narcissistic personality described by Bursten (1986) best fits individuals with pathological consumer behaviors. It should be clear by now that the category Bursten calls "the craving personality" comes closest to those with pleonexia. The "orally tinged" behaviors of this personality type, feelings of inner hunger needing to be filled by objects, as well as the "driven quality" of this dependent behavior best describes the pleonexic. However, Bursten's disclaimer notwithstanding, his nosology is greatly limited by the gender bias in his sampling. Specifically, his male clients show a more aggressive form of self-expression than has been traditionally allowed to females in our and most societies.

(2) *Manic Episode* —some of the criteria of manic episode may be associated with compulsive buying and spending, especially during shopping binges. Factors such as a high, exaggerated self-esteem or pretentiousness, and, of course, over involvement in behaviors that elicit short-term pleasure, while having a strong likelihood of producing long-term negative consequences. In fact, it was here that the 1987 *DSM* included uncontrolled bouts of splurging.[25] It is interesting to note the similarity with the lack of insight that usually accompanies an

acute manic episode.[26] However, except when the two disorders coexist the differential diagnosis can be made by noting the absence of the other features of bipolar disorder in many individuals who engage in pathological consumer behavior.

(3) *Antisocial Personality Disorder* —as noted earlier, some individuals with pathological consumer behavior may also be involved in behaviors associated with antisocial personality disorder (one thinks, for example, of some hoarders of animals). Also, as noted, any antisocial activities these individuals perform are usually not violent, and are associated with the acquisition of money, or commodities, as well as the disregarding or breaking of financial contracts..

Diagnostic Criteria for Pleonexia

I have already noted that, after years of study and some contention, hoarding disorder was added to the fifth edition of the DSM in 2013 as a distinct condition. It is not necessary to present the criteria here, as they are readily available. However, there is still no category of compulsive buying, therefore, the diagnostic criteria that I suggested for pleonexia in 1989 are still relevant today, and should be given here:

Dysfunctional buying, acquiring, and spending behavior, accompanied by these specific components:

(1) The person engages in chronic acquiring.

(2) An increase in emotional response immediately before shopping or acquiring of objects, feelings of pleasure or relief while acquiring, followed by anxiety and/or remorse.

(3) A feeling of lack of control during or following incidents of acquiring.

(4) Obsession with spending money or acquiring objects and with all aspects of commodities.

(5) Recurrent spending of amounts of money beyond a person's capacity, or purchasing more expensive or greater quantities of goods than intended.

(6) Perpetuation of such behavior despite the inability to pay mounting debts, or despite other significant social, occupational, relationship, or legal problems that the person knows to be exacerbated by such spending.

(7) Agitation or moodiness if prevented from acquiring or spending.

(8) Resulting inability to meet economic burdens, such as payments on loans, rent or failing to provide support for dependents.

(9) Multiple failed efforts to reduce or stop such spending behaviors.

Treatment Recommendations

Consistent with the overdetermined character of pleonexia, this book has utilized a multidimensional analysis, or what the anthropologist Clifford Geertz calls "thick description" of multiple interacting factors in its etiology. Consonant with this perspective is a multimodal and holistic approach to treatment (see the similar analysis and rationale for treatment of anorexia in Garfinkel and Garner, 1982). One of the strong attractions to social work practice, for me personally, has been its historical openness to this holistic approach, including consideration of social, cultural, and even political factors in the diagnosis and treatment of pathological behavior. As I have argued here, this approach is especially important when dealing with problems relating to our consumer culture. One early model of social work practice that attempts to take such an "ecological" and contextual perspective is the "life model" of Carel Germain and Alex Gitterman (1980). Their model takes an "integrated" or systems view of complex problems similar to the consumer pathology described in this book. Their model sees all of life as a process of "adaptation and reciprocal interaction between people and their social and physical environments."[27] The percolation of different levels of influence through the personality is an interactive process that requires both an ecological analysis, as well as a multifaceted approach to treatment. Such a model assumes the fundamental social and political nature of clients and their problems, and what Charles

235

Horton Cooley distinguished as their "*carnal, social, and spiritual* consciousness."[28] Another assumption is that there is a synergistic effect that comes from combining different intervention strategies and adapting them to the different needs of a diverse population with multiple problems. The goal of therapy is to help encourage the growth of capacities to address maladaptive patterns of behavior.

An especially egregious example of the opposite, or reductionist, approach can be found in Gad Saad's *The Consuming Instinct.*[29] Although he acknowledges that compulsive buying and hoarding are "technically" different disorders, he argues that compulsive buyers can be characterized as hoarders of meaningful products, especially items promoted as enhancing the individual's physical appearance. He uses this conjecture to explain why the vast majority of compulsive buyers are women. He asserts that this is confirming evidence for his general explanation of behaviors that appear illogical as actually forms of Darwinian adaptation and evolution.[30] Saad ignores or is unaware of evidence that hoarding disorder is more prevalent in males. But, a more serious issue is the limitations of his argument for treatment and prevention of these disorders. A much more fruitful application of the evidence for the prevalence of women with compulsive buying can be found from the similarities in the comprehensive approach outlined here and certain key tenets of female-oriented therapies. Feminist inspired methods were developed in the 1980s with increasing sophistication to help women to see the role played by cultural and

236

sociopolitical forces and their specific behaviors.[31] I noted in 1989 that one prominent symptom of pleonexia, namely low self-esteem, could be seen as both the result and the perpetuation of external oppression in a patriarchal society. Joel Kovel had called attention to the use of various techniques of therapy and "praxis" that had evolved to replace the lack of an authentic community and the artificial split between public and private aspects of being in our society.[32] Two such techniques developed and refined by feminist therapists were: consciousness raising (CR) groups, and therapeutic self help or peer groups. The first of these was arguably best defined by Juliet Mitchell as, "the process of transforming the hidden, individual fears of people into a shared awareness of the meaning of them as social problems."[33] There are many historical examples of oppressed peoples finding emotional relief or catharsis from a shared understanding of the subtle, unnatural, political forces that have led them to act against their own self-interest or in unhealthy ways. Note that there are two dialectical aspects to this process: (1) using individual understanding about self as a basis for analyzing shared oppression; and (2) using understanding of oppression as an aid to individual understanding. Essential to the philosophy and application of this process is its *dialectical* nature (this is a concept borrowed from Martin Buber).[34]. The power of such a process comes in large part from a communicative relationship based on mutual respect, empowerment, and nonhierarchical equality.[35] The second technique mentioned —the therapeutic self help or peer

237

group —is also based on peer equality and mutual empathy.[36] This approach, labeled "inspirational group therapy" by Alvin Scodel, is a feminist adaptation to a clinical setting of the self help movement.[37] Since I first suggested the use of such groups as "spender menders" and "debtors anonymous," there has been an increase in both self help and peer support groups, especially for hoarders. The negative feelings, such as shame and embarrassment, caused, in part, by social and family reactions to hoarding behavior, for example, can be transformed by the mutual understanding, encouragement, and empowerment that results from a shared community of sufferers. These peer support groups can sometimes be led by clients who act as trained facilitators. The use of peer facilitators who have been through a recovery program, and have gained some insight into the many facets of this disorder, as well as basic training in group process, appears to give the best treatment outcomes. This team approach to therapy is most effective when it is coupled with family support groups and community education to address the many misconceptions that have usually led to ineffective, often counter-effective, attempts at dealing with hoarding behavior. Central to all of these group and communal techniques is the greater emphasis placed on fostering interdependence and social support; something that can carry over into individual psychodynamic and CBT clinical sessions.

Some involvement with such a community would appear to be a necessary adjunct to individual and clinician led group therapy because of the peculiar problems of avoiding any

238

compulsive behavior in a society that strongly promotes such behavior. One added problem is the widely documented tendency to substitute one addictive behavior for another.[38] To the extent that pleonexia expresses an underlying dispositional disorder, then change of one addictive behavior represents what Roy Schafer calls a change in "content," as opposed to a change in "structure."[39] Another problem, one shared with eating disorders and particularly strong in our culture, is the impossibility of total abstinence from the addictive behavior, since acquiring, shopping, and spending money are a necessity in our society. Since complete avoidance of reinforcing behaviors and environmental cues is unlikely, individuals will need the kind of ongoing support that can come from a peer community and a sponsor. An additional benefit from involvement with a self help community is noted by several feminist therapists, namely, that character can sometimes be changed by involvement in social actions, even regardless of the outcome of such attempts to change society.[40] For example, the community of sufferers from consumer pathologies may attempt to bring about some change in the way that the advertising and marketing industry nourishes addictive behaviors. The benefits that can come from channeling anger, increasing self-esteem, empowerment, and greater community empathy have been demonstrated, even in situations where such political efforts are not successful.

Another powerful technique that I recommended for the treatment of consumer pathology has undergone considerable improvement since 1989. I had been impressed by the work of Mary Bergner and her associates, combining "feminist therapy tenets," with the cognitive restructuring principles of "rational behavioral therapy" and social learning theory in order to help women "restructure their sex-role stereotyped thoughts and feelings about their bodies in ways that were useful to them."[41] I noted that similar methods had been effectively used to enhance self-esteem with eating disorders. Bergner's structured groups combined visual and kinesthetic techniques to help participants master "*how* their internalized, culturally derived self-statements led to personal feelings of worthlessness" (p. 25, emphasis in original). I added that cognitive restructuring, homework assignments, journal keeping, and group processing of content were used to foster self-worth independent of body image, and that such self-enhancement tools would strengthen resistance to the effects of consumer marketing. I added that a strong educational component was utilized in all of these approaches to treatment, in order to help the client see the wider, harmful consequences of giving in to these kinds of cultural forces influencing her behavior. I compared this to what family systems therapists called the "context." The goals of feminist therapy in the 70s and 80s, especially "the humanist goal of emotional growth," and "the ultimate goal of women developing a sense of our personal and political power," remain essential for therapy with sufferers from consumer pathology.[42] The question of personal freedom has been a major issue throughout this book. Every form of compulsive behavior ultimately ends up restricting freedom, and to that extent at least is "bad."[43] However, the specific goals of treatment for the compulsions associated with consumer behavior have the substantial advantage that they reflect the wisdom of every great religious leader since the Axial Age, every great moral philosopher of both East and West, and, now, the experimental findings of modern science. All of this collective wisdom, as well as the scientific findings converge on the same understanding: that a flourishing and healthy human life is only possible when the goods that come from human relationships are allowed to flourish, free of the tyranny of consumer values.[44]

I noted that many of these same methods and principles could be applied in individual therapy as well, referring to Brodsky (1976) and Lerman (1976) for examples. I concluded my 1989 work with the acknowledgement that a good deal of more research needed to be done on all aspects of pleonexia, including: (1) genetic and predisposing factors (perhaps along the lines of Daniel Stern's analysis of "personal things" in infancy; (2) a feminist critical analysis of cultural nourishing factors; and, (3) the whole question of treatment methods.[45] Of course, all of the treatment methods available have undergone major refinement and improvement in recent decades. I will conclude here by briefly mentioning a few more of these refinements in treatment.

Therapists who work with individuals with substance use problems soon learn that a frontal attack against a client's denial system, especially early in treatment, is almost always counterproductive. However, the important work on stages of change, by James Prochaska and Carlo DiClemente and their colleagues, built on this awareness and added both a theoretical framework and practice guidelines to help therapists motivate clients for positive change. There is not room here for a meaningful summary of their work, and this information is readily available. Suffice it to say that this work, especially the refinements made to the first, *precontemplation,* stage will prove highly useful for treatment of compulsive consumer behavior, especially with hoarding problems. As noted earlier in this book, related work on "motivational interviewing" has added a powerful tool to address client ambivalence, a central feature of the second, *contemplation,* stage of change. Again, this is a refinement of methods that many substance use disorder therapists learned from trial and error work with high denial clients. The basis of this technique goes all the way back to Socratic, open-ended, but at the same time directive, questioning. But, there is also growing neurological evidence about human learning that, at least in part, explains its efficacy. It has the substantial added benefit of showing the same kind of respect and empathy for the client as the other methods recommended here, by normalizing behavior, as well as by building confidence, in a collaborative endeavor to bring about change. There isn't room here to give examples of the method.[46] Suffice it to say that the respectful and positive feedback of this method can be especially useful in an in-home or clinic, clean out exercise with a client with hoarding disorder. Also, a growing

242

awareness of the importance of "case conceptualization" to the effectiveness of cognitive behavioral therapy has led to the development of a very useful "collaborative" model, one that has strong similarities to the treatment methods I have recommended earlier in this chapter.[47] Finally, Gail Steketee, Randy Frost, and Christiana Bratiotis, among others, have developed a series of therapist guides and client work books, most published by Oxford Press, that constitute an essential resource for anyone dealing, directly or indirectly, with hoarding problems.

Problems directly related to the growing tyranny of market values over every sphere of human life have caused immense personal suffering. It is my hope that the analysis presented in this book will contribute to the healing of our society and its citizens.

Notes

[1] Dittmar, 2008, p.55

[2] Foucault, 2009, pp.143-4

[3] Cushman, 1990, 1995; Conrad, 1992; Lee and Mysyk, 2004

[4] Ignatieff, 1984, pp.62-4

[5] Nussbaum, 1994, 2004

[6] Miller, 2014

[7] Roberts, 2012, p.86

[8] "acquisitive disorders" has been used, see, Aboujaoude, 2010

[9] cf. Hampshire, 1971, pp.34-41; McAdams, 2009 on 'dispositions.' I follow Alasdair MacIntyre in arguing that 'greed,' the most common translation for pleonexia, should be seen as naming a "desire," to be distinguished from the disposition; see Balot, 2001, p.33

[10] Balot, 2001, p.7

[11] Hadot, 1995, p.83

[12] Krueger, 1988, p.576

[13] Spencer, 2013

[14] Neu, 1977; Mitchell and Aron, 1999

[15] Tolin, et al., 2009; Fitch, 2011

[16] Nussbaum, 1994; North, 1966

[17] Elster, 1999, p.198

[18] Lukes, 1974, pp.23, 34

[19] Fitzgerald, 1977

[20] 1980, p.1

[21] Cushman, 1990, p. 609

[22] Keynes, 1930/1963, pp.358–371

[23] Cushman, 1995; Fancher, 1998; Woolfolk, 1997

[24] Arnold, 1960; Nussbaum, 2001

1. The All-Consuming Self

[1] McCracken, 1990

[2] "On the Basis of Morality"

[3] *World as will and reality*. 2, 638

[4] Bellegarde and Potenza, 2010

[5] Hirschman, 2002; Scitovsky, 1992

[6] Heilbroner, 1980; Stout, 1988; Bellah et al., 1992; Boundy, 1993

[7] Grant, Potenza, Weinstein, et al., 2010

[8] Shaffer, 1997

[9] see, for example, Faber, et al., 1995

[10] 1958, p.121
[11] Dittmar, 1992; Elliott, 1994; Ritchins, 1994; Kasser and Kanner, 2004
[12] Black, 2001; Black, 2009
[13] Müller, et al., 2001
[14] Steketee, Frost, & Kyrios, 2003
[15] Petry and Madden, 2010, p.337
[16] see, for example, Goldman et al., 2010; for an exception, see, Elster and Skog, 1999, 25-6.
[17] Mischel, 2014;Ainslie, 1992, 2001
[18] Valverde, 1998, p.2
[19] Loewenstien, 1996
[20] p.306
[21] no.6, p.9
[22] Vohs and Baumeister, 2013, pp.538-9; these ideas will be examined below
[23] see Kennett, 2001, for an excellent discussion of this point
[24] Gardner, 1985; Rook and Gardner 1993
[25] 2013, pp.540-1
[26] Tice, Bratslavsky & Baumeister, 2001
[27] Gilbert, Gill, & Wilson, 2002, p.441
[28] 2011, p.402
[29] 1996, 1999, 2001
[30] see Damasio, 1999, for background on feeling and emotions
[31] Messiha, 1993; the positive effects of medication will be examined in the concluding chapter
[32] 1999, pp.236-7
[33] Faber &Vohs, 2004
[34] Tice, Bratslavsky, & Baumeister, 2001
[35] Kacen & Lee, 2002
[36] Kivetz and Keinan, 2006; Keinan and Kivetz, 2008
[37] Claes, et al., 2010; Carver & Scheier, 1981 has a positive take on loops
[38] 1988, p.574
[39] Tversky & Kahneman, 1981
[40] Keinan and Kivetz, 2008, p.676
[41] Balot, 2001, p.38
[42] e.g., Schlosser, Black, Repertinger, and Freet, 1994; Black, 2001, 2007
[43] e.g., Scherhorn, 1990; Sohn and Choi, 2012
[44] O'Guinn and Faber, 1989; Faber and Christenson, 1996
[45] Baumeister, et al., 1994
[46] Ingham, 1989, especially, pp.123-5
[47] American Psychiatric Association, 3rd edition, revised, pp.321-8
[48] Dagher, 2007
[49] Beatty & Ferrell, 1998
[50] Elliott, 1994;Koran et al., 2006

[51] Hartston, 2012; for a critique of the medicalization approach, see, Conrad, 1992; Hollander & Allen, 2006

[52] Ruden, 1997, p.149; Morino, et al., 2011

[53] Richards, 2000

[54] Rook, 1987, pp.194-5

[55] see Winstine, 1985, for a good example of the latter

[56] compare, Leiss, 1976

[57] Bardo, 1985-6; for a later summary, see Bordo, 1992

[58] Peele, 1985;Rook, 1987; see, Rook and Fisher, 1995; for an update, see, Murunganantham and Bhakat, 2013

[59] Krueger, 1988, p.574; Rook, 1987

[60] Glatt and Cook, 1987, p.1257; see, e.g., Krueger, 1988; Dittmar, 1992, 2005; Elliott, 1994

[61] 2001, p.16

[62] Mitchell, et al., 2006, p.1864

[63] Cushman, 1990; Benson, 2000, Dittmar, 2001

[64] 2001, p.243

[65] Koran, et al. 2006

[66] Tolin, et al., 2010

[67] Johnson, et al., 2011, p. 651

[68] Roberts and Tanner, 2000; Roberts and Jones, 2001; Roberts and Pirog, 2004

[69] Seung-Hee, Lennon, and Rudd, 2000; Lennon, Sanik, and Stanforth, 2003

[70] Faber and O'Guinn, 1988; Faber and Vohs, 2013; Steketee and Frost, 2003

[71] Frost, Marten, Lahart, & Rosenblate, 1990

[72] Mueller, et al., 2007, 2009; Steketee and Frost, 2003

[73] Black, 2007

[74] O'Guinn and Faber, 1989; Faber and O'Guinn, 1992

[75] 1997, p.652; Lears, 1983, was among the first to show this link between the therapeutic community and advertising; also, see Tye, 1998; Cushman, 1990

[76] Caspary, 2000; Sen, 1985; Nussbaum, 2003

[77] Faber, 2011, p. 4;Black, 2001, 2007

[78] Lejoyeux and Weinstein, 2010

[79] Frost and Steketee, 2010, pp.46-51

[80] de Vries, 2008, p.23; this will be examined further in the next chapter

[81] McElroy, Phillips, & Keck, 1994; Frost and Hartl, 1996; Frost et al., 1998

[82] 1991; 1994

[83] 2008, p.30; also see, Timpano, et al., 2011

[84] Steketee, Frost, & Kyrios, 2003

[85] (Frost, Steketee, & Williams, 2000; Coles et al., 2003

[86] Prochaska, Norcross & Diclemente, 2007

[87] Patronek, 1999; Fost, Steketee, & Williams, 2000; Frost, Patronek, & Rosenfield, 2011

[88] Donnelly, 1983

246

[89] Sander, 1943, p.155

[90] 1951, p.297

[91] 1986, pp.549-78

[92] Clark, Mankikar, and Gray, 1975; for a critique, see Giovanni, et al., 2013

[93] Snowdon, Halliday, and Banerjee, 2013

[94] 2010, p.39

[95] Thaler, 1980

[96] Kahneman, Knetsch, & Thaler, 1990; Kahneman, 2011; Ariely, 2009

[97] 2011, p.295

[98] 2000, p.58

[99] 1994, pp.71-7

[100] Saxena, 2008

[101] Tolin, 2011;Tolin, et al., 2012

[102] see, for example, Grisham, et al., 2010

[103] Knutson, et al., 2008

[104] Frost and Steketee, 2011, 12-13

[105] 5th edition, 2013, 235-51

[106] Steketee & Frost, 2013

[107] Miller & Rollnick, 2013

[108] 2011, p.17

[109] 2005, pp.48, 154; Kahneman, 1999, pp.13-14

[110] p.49

[111] Oldham, Hollander, and Skodol, 1996, ix

[112] e.g., Faber, 2001

[113] 2001, p.156

[114] p.158

[115] see the chapters in Vohs & Baumeister, 2011

[116] Ross, Kincaid, Spurrett, and Collins, 2010

[117] there is not enough room here to go into all the problems with the medical model; see, for example, Kincaid and Sullivan, 2010; Fingarette, 1988; Peele, 1989

[118] Voh & Baumeister, 2011, p.543

[119] see the essays in Elster and Skog, 1999

[120] Kasser, 2002, p.57; see also, Kasser and Kanner, 2004; Dittmar and Bond, 2005

[121]Roberts & Pirog, 2004

[122] for further evidence, see Hoch and Loewenstein, 1991; E. Hirschman, 1992

[123] for a good summary, see Ali Khalidi, 1993

[124] Levy, 2013; Sadler, 2005

2. The All-Consuming Society

[1] Freud, 1913, pp. 143–4

[2] Bordo, 1985 –6; Lasch, 1979, p. 34)

[3] see, *e.g.,* Germain & Gitterman, 1980; Soloman, 1986; Leonard, 1984

[4] Rieff, 1966, p. 372

[5] 1984, pp. 136-41;Lasch, 1979, p. 34, 1984, p. 25

[6] Levin, 1985, p. 5

[7] Jacoby, 1980, p. 60

[8] Garter & Edwards, 1988, p. 76

[9] Orford, 1985, p. 321

[10] Reich, 1946/1970, p. XXLL

[11] Reich, 1946/1970, 1973; the phrase comes from Borneman, 1976, p. 11

[12] 1984, p. 137, 1988, pp. 1112; Webster, 1986, p. 1740

[13] Liddell & Scott, 1953, p. 1416

[14] MacIntyre, 1984, p. 137, emphasis in original

[15] MacIntyre, 1988, pp. 111-12)

[16] MacIntyre, 1988, p. 112; Jerry Muller translates pleonexia with the evocative "overreaching," 2003, p.5

[17] MacIntyre, 1965, pp. 55-60; cf., Helene Deutsch, 1965 for another example see Ryle, 1949, pp. 83-153

[18] MacIntyre, 1965, p.59

[19] Alston, 1967, p. 406

[20] 1949, pp. 83-153

[21] 1972, pp. 423-44

[22] Alston, 1967, p. 404

[23] Alston, 1967, p. 404

[24] Alston, 1967, p. 406

[25] 1965, p. 59

[26] cf., Coblentz, 1965 for a history of this difference

[27] 1989, pp.211-302

[28] 2001, p.28, n.16, emphasis in original

[29] 2004, p.277

[30] Coblentz, 1965, p. v

[31] Fromm, 1964, p. 179

[32] Levin, 1987, p. 65

[33] Douglas & Isherwood, 1979; Herskovitz, 1960; Coblentz, 1965

[34] Wilden, 1984, p. 20

[35] Douglas & Isherwood, 1979, pp. 131137

[36] Coblentz, 1965, pp. 7−9

[37] Taussig, 1980

[38] Taussig, 1965, pp. 35 −37

[39] Baudrillard, 1970; in Baudrillard, 1981, he finds both the Marxist and psychoanalytic "myths" of the subject to be inadequate - Baudrillard's work will be examined at the end of this chapter

[40] Campbell, 1987

[41] Leiss, et al., 1986, 264-296; cf. also, Marx's distinction between "use-value" and "exchange-value" in Schneider & Wilson, 1975

[42] see Ferenczi's unfortunate term "capitalistic instinct" - Borneman, 1976, p. 46; this misuse of 'instinct', and the related notion of "true/false needs" will be further critiqued below

[43] Campbell, 1987, pp. 42 −45

[44] Campbell 1987, p. 237n30; Campbell, 1987, p. 44

[45] Campbell follows Wallach & Wallach, 1989, 196−225; see also the excellent critique of the neo-Freudian concept of true/false needs in Sringborg, 1981, chapters. 8 & 9

[46] see, for example, Nielson, 1977

[47] Mataix-Cols, et al., 2010; Nordsletten, et al., 2013

[48] 1890, p.279

[49] Campbell, like Baudrillard, 1970, uses Vance Packard and John K. Galbraith as prime examples; however Packard 1957 gave many humorous examples of how advertisements failed in their attempt to manipulate consumers

[50] 1987, p. 48

[51] see Leiss et al., 1986, pp. 33 −38 for more arguments against manipulationism

[52] Campbell, 1987, pp. 49 −57

[53] See his classic *Theory of the Leisure Class* was published in 1899, just one year before Freud's *Interpretation of* Dreams; for a work which explores the interesting parallels between Freud and Veblen, see Schneider, 1948

[54] economists now term these "Veblen effects" on consumer behavior; and they include 'bandwagon' effects and 'snob appeal' as examples - see Baudrillard, 1981, pp. 205−210

[55] Galbraith, 1958, p. 125; Campbell notes that 'getting ahead of the Joneses' is closer to Veblen than the formula usually associated with his name— viz. 'keeping up with the Joneses' - Campbell, 1987, p. 239n58

[56] Riesman, 1953, p. 60

[57] Schneider, 1948, p. 86n96

[58] Campbell, 1987, p. 51

[59] Campbell, 1987, p. 52; Schneider, 1948, pp. 85 −94 shows how this aspect of Veblen's theory was derived from the 'instinctivist' psychology of his day. Schneider offers a further critique of 'instinctivism'

[60] Campbell, 1987, p. 53

[61] 1987, pp. 55-56; Campbell, 1991; Campbell, 1995

[62] Campbell, 1987, p. 55

[63] Campbell, 1987, pp. 86 −87

[64] Delattre, 1986, p. 135

[65] among the most prominent being Herbert Marcuse who wrote of our "self-subjugation" and our "consumption repression" —Marcuse, 1964, p. 108, 1968

[66] Lasch, 1984, p. 27n.

[67] Simon, 1974, 1976

[68] Simon, 1976, p. 369)

[69] Durkheim, 1897/1971, pp.246-254

[70] Simon, 1976, p. 367

[71] Simon, 1976, p. 371

[72] Simon, 1976, p. 372

[73] Simon, 1974, p. 145, 1976, p .375

[74] Ewen, 1988; cf., also, Ewen 1977, and Ewen & Ewen, 1982

[75] Ewen, 1988, pp. 102, 72

[76] Ewen, 1977

[77] Ewen, 1988, p. 105

[78] Simmel, 1907/1978; Simmel, 1971a.

[79] Simmel, 1907/1978 — an important exception is Marx's "psychological footnote" analyzed by Anthony Wilden, 1984, pp. 29-30, 251-255 - more on this below).

[80] Simmel, 1907/1978, p. 239

[81] *blasierteit* - Simmel, 1907, p. 265

[82] Simmel, 1971b, pp. 329-30 - this is an anticipation of the important notion of "fatigue" in addictions research to be examined later

[83] Marx's exchange or abstract value - Simmel, 1907/1978, pp. 255–6

[84] *der Geize* - Simmel, 1907, pp. 253–4

[85] Simmel, 1907/1978, p. 351, Simmel 1971a

[86] Simmel 1907/1978, p.255; compare Simon on "conummatory repression" above Simmel, 1907/1978, pp. 479 –481

[87] *die Begierde und Hingabe,* literally, longing and devotion; the common word for addiction is *Sucht* - Simmel, 1908, p. 314

[88] 1978, p.279

[89] see the excellent discussion in Poggi, 1993

[90] Baudrillard 1968, 1970

[91] *valeur d'échange signe* - Baudrillard, 1981, pp. 66 –67

[92] an analogous linguistic turn toward increasing levels of semiotic abstraction can be seen in family theory

[93] ("*les besoins empiriques*" - Baudrillard, 1970, pp. 93 105

[94] Baudrillard, 1981, pp. 130 –142

[95] Baudrillard, 1981, p. 63

[96] Baudrillard, 1970, pp.97- 99, emphasis in original; 1998, p.72

[97] Baudrillard, 1970, p. 100; 1998, p.73

[98] Springborg 1981 in her critique of Reich, Fromm, and Marcuse offers further arguments against the Marxian true/false needs distinction

[99] *vitrine* -Baudrillard 1970, p. 102; 1998, p.74

[100] - Baudrillard, 1970, p. 112, emphasis in original; 1998, p.80

[101] Baudrillard, 1970, p. 104 - emphasis in original; 1998, p.75

[102] Baudrillard, 1970, p. 105, 1998, p.76; see also, 1968, p. 219

[103] Baudrillard, 1970, p. 107

[104] ("*manqué*" namely, "the *desire for social meaning*"- Baudrillard, 1970, p. 108 - emphasis in original; 1998, pp.77 –78

[105] Baudrillard, 1970, pp. 109-113; 1998, pp.78 −86

[106] Baudrillard, 1981, p. 54

[107] (*"une simple constraint de prestige"*- Baudrillard, 1968, p. 238

[108] Baudrillard, 1968, pp. 232 −239; elsewhere he calls advertising and consumption "the cold seduction" of objects, quoted in Racevskis 1983, pp. 158   −159)

[109] Baudrillard, 1968, pp. 226

[110] Baudrillard, 1968, pp. 189 −190

[111] (Baudrillard, 1981, p. 67   — emphasis in the original

[112] Baudrillard, 1968, especially, pp. 153−160

[113] see, Baudrillard, 1981b for a summary article of his critique; both in Baudrillard 1976, p. 8 and in 1979, he elaborates on his view of "the death of psychoanalysis"

[114] Raceviskis, 1983, p. 163; see Rochberg-Halton, 1986, pp. 95. for a similar criticism of Baudrillard's "tendency to sunder meaning from experience", Rochberg-Halton, 1986, p. 59

[115] Leiss, 1976

[116] 1976, p. 14

[117] Leiss, 1976, p. 16

[118] Leiss, 1976, p. 18

[119] Leiss, 1976, p. 19

[120] Leiss, 1976, p. 25

[121] Schachter, 1971

[122] Leiss, 1976, p. 25

[123] Leiss, 1976, p. 26

[124] Leiss, 1976, p. 27

[125] Leiss, 1976, p. 25

[126] Leiss, 1976, pp. 66, 74; here he takes issue with Baudrillard, who maintains a mistaken belief that the symbolic can be separated from its material base

[127] (Leiss, 1976, p. 67

[128] Leiss, 1976, p. 85, emphasis in original

[129] Arendt, 1959, p.110

[130] Leiss, 1976, p. 90

[131] Leiss, 1976, p. 93

[132] Leiss, et al., 2005, p.215

[133] Leiss, et al., 2005, pp.326−329

[134] Kovel, 1982, p. 106

3. All-Consuming Desire

[1] e.g. James Mitchell et al., 2008; Steketee, Frost, & Kyrios, 2003

[2] Frost & Hartl, 1996

[3] Freud, 1954, p. 244

[4] Abraham, 1925/1948, p. 417

[5] cf., MacIntyre, 1959, pp. 50   −70; Ricoeur, 1970, pp. 8714; Izenberg, 1976, pp. 108   −165; Schafer, 1976, pp. 223   342

[6] MacIntyre, 1958, p. 51

[7] cf., e.g., Toulman, 1948; Flew, 1954 — Flew was to later modify his position in Flew, 1956

[8] it is this rewriting of Freud that Adolf Grilnbaum criticizes as "the hermeneutic version of psychoanalysis"; Grunbaum, 1984, pp. 1-95; more on Grunbaum below

[9] Wittgenstein, 1980, p. 33

[10] Wittgenstein, 1967, p. 41; see, e.g., Freud, 1915, pp. 271–272

[11] For a reply by a psychoanalyst to these criticisms, as well as an analysis of Freud's "scientific" use of disposition terms, cf., Frenkel-Brunswik, 1954 — especially, pp. 278–279

[12] MacIntyre, 1958, p. 59

[13] Frenkel-Brunswik, 1954, p. 279; cf., Shope, 1970, for further critique of Frenkel-Brunswik on disposition terms in psychoanalysis

[14] Rubinstein, 1967, p. 37

[15] MacIntyre, 1958, pp. 56-7; cf., Frenkel-Brunswik, 1954, pp. 320 –324, for more on this role of the concept of self-deception in psychoanalysis

[16] MacIntyre, 1958, pp. 54 –55

[17] Grunbaum, 1984, pp. 25 –30, emphasis original

[18] 1983, pp. 241 242

[19] Hampshire, 1962, pp. 59 –68

[20] Freud, 1912, p. 431; also such "mental acts" as dreams and parapraxes — Freud, 1915, p. 265

[21] MacIntyre, 1958, p. 52

[22] Peters, 1960, p. 53

[23] Peters, 1960, p. 62

[24] MacIntyre, 1958, p. 60

[25] Flew, 1954, p. 8

[26] Rapaport, 1967, pp. 853 –915

[27] Rapaport, 1967, pp. 862 –863

[28] Rapaport, 1967, p. 883

[29] Rapaport, 1967, pp. 865 –866; these categories will prove useful defining pleonexia

[30] namely, pressure, source, aim, and object — cf., Laplanche & Pontalis, 1973, p. 21

[31] Freud, 1895a, pp. 357 –376; Freud, 1895a, p. 360

[32] Freud, 1895a, p. 367

[33] cf., Laplanche & Pontalis, 1973, pp. 292 –293

[34] cf., e.g., Freud & Breuer, 1895b, pp. 241–242; cf., Breuer's contribution to Freud & Breuer, 1895a; Freud, 1916-17, pp. 234 –235

[35] 1973, pp. 318 –319; Laplanche & Pontalis, 1968, p. 1

[36] 1988, pp. 33 –42

[37] as Laplanche & Pontalis, 1973 note a number of times; cf., e.g., p. 131

[38] quoted in Grunbaum, 1984, pp. 5, 10

[39] Bettleheim, 1983, p. 93

[40] Goldberg, 1988, p. 17

[41] Bettleheim, 1983, pp. 104–105

[42] Bettleheim, 1983, pp. 41 –42

[43] Freud, 1933, especially, pp. 187 –190

[44] Freud, 1933, lecture 35, pp. 191 −192, 195; main in below

[45] Hartmann 1927

[46] Hartmann, 1927, p. 376—"understandable" is the translator's term for *verstehende* which is more commonly rendered, by the hermeneutician's for example, as "meaningful"

[47] Hartmann, 1927, p. 375

[48] Hartmann, 1927, p. 377

[49] Hartmann, 1927, p. 378

[50] MacIntyre, 1958, p. 63

[51] Freud, 1901, pp. 239−279

[52] cf., McGrath, 1986, pp. 111 −127

[53] Dreyfus, 1987, pp. 69−70; the term 'representation' is a rendering of *Vorstellung* and *Vorstellungrepräentant,* usually translated as 'idea'; but actually they are technical terms from German 'intentionalist' philosophy − cf., Laplanche & Pontalis,1973, pp. 200 −201, 203−205

[54] Edleson, 1988, p. 248; Edelson's example is the "wish-fulfillment"

[55] Rief, 1961, p.29

[56] Wolff, 1988, p.35, emphasis in original; cf. Hempel, 1965, pp.437−445

[57] quoted in Suppe, 1977, p. 670, emphasis in original

[58] Lacan, 1968, p. 55

[59] in the sense of *überdeutung,* cf., Laplanche & Pontalis, 1973, pp. 292 −294 for examples of this use of the concept

[60] Laplanche & Pontalis, 1973, p. 292

[61] 1967, p. 867

[62] 1927, p. 383

[63] Hartmann, 1927, p. 392

[64] Freud, 1915, p. 266; cf. Sulloway, 1983, pp. 48, 50 −51

[65] quoted in Rapaport, 1967, p. 870

[66] Freud, 1915, p. 164

[67] Hartmann, 1927, p. 393

[68] Hartman, 1927, pp.376, 389; "understandable" is one translation of *verstehende,* more commonly rendered as "meaningful.'

[69] Hartmann, 1927, p. 394

[70] compare Hartmann, 1927, p.395 with Hartmann, 1960

[71] cf., Jones, 1953, p. 366; also Sulloway, 1983, *passim* — Sulloway notes Freud's continued ambivalence toward biology

[72] Hartmann, 1927, p. 400

[73] Hartmann, 1927, p. 402; for an excellent discussion of the role of purposive interpretations in psychology, cf., Boden, 1978

[74] quoted in Edelson, 1988, p. 270

[75] cf., Edelson, 1988, p. 252 for Edelson on Freud's use of 'cause'

[76] Grünbaum, 1984; Grünbaum examines Habermas, the early Ricoeur, G.S. Klein, and R. Schafer; for a very recent collection on hermeneutics and psychoanalysis, cf., Messer, Sass, & Woolfolk, 1988

[77] Shope quoted in Grünbaum, 1984, p.67, emphasis in original; see Shope, 1973 and 1985; this is a different use of 'sign' than the one given by Jones in his famous article on the "Theory of Symbolism"—see, Jones, 1961, p.88

[78] Griinbaum, 1984, p. 69

[79] Grunbaum, 1984, p. 70,emphasis in original. The Freud quotes are from Freud, 1910, p. 38

[80] Freud, 1912, p. 37

[81] Freud, 1912, p. 39

[82] Grünbaum, 1984, p. 71; the German word *Motiv* is derived directly from the word *Motion*

[83] Ludwig Binswanger as quoted in Izenberg, 1976, pp. 136–138; for Binswanger's statement of the 'reasons vs. causes' thesis cf., e.g., Binswanger, 1968, pp. 156 –158

[84] Izenberg, 1976, p. 136

[85] Izenberg, 1976, p. 136

[86] cf., Skidelsky, 2010, pp.139—140 for an example

[87] Izenberg, 1976, p. 136, emphasis in original

[88] Quoted in Izenberg, 1976, p. 137, emphasis in original

[89] Izenberg, 1976, p. 137

[90] Izenberg, 1976, p. 137

[91] Freud, 1908, pp. 203–209

[92] Freud, 1908, p. 203

[93] Freud, 1908, p. 204; in Freud, 1905

[94] cf., especially, pp. 140 –141

[95] Freud, 1908, p. 205; also, Freud, 1905, pp. 79, 140

[96] , 1973, pp. 431 –434

[97] Freud, 1913, pp. 442–52, 499; also introduced in Freud, 1905, pp. 78, 79, 140

[98] cf., Laplanche & Pontalis, 1973, pp. 377   –378

[99] Fenichel, 1945, p. 151; the German suffix *bildung* holds an important place in literary history, with its connotation of sophisticated cultivation

[100] A. Freud, 1936; Freud, 1937, p. 80; Laplanche & Pontalis, 1973, pp. 25   –26

[101] A. Freud1936, p. 33; Reich's ideas will be examined later in this chapter

[102] A. Freud, 1936, p. 33

[103] Laplanche & Pontalis, 1973, p. 25

[104] Freud, 1937, pp. 64–65

[105] , pp. 357 –376

[106] Freud, 1937, p. 64 —'*erworbene*' carries a meaning of 'loss' in the business sense, and *ungünstige* carries a meaning of 'malignity'

[107] Freud, 1937/1963b, p. 238

[108] Rapaport, 1967, pp. 864   –86Freud, 1937/1963b, p. 253

[109] Rapaport, 1967, p. 864

[110] 1937/1963b, p. 253

[111] see, in particular, Freud, 1915, p. 210

[112] Freud, 1926, pp. 122, 148; Laplanche & Pontalis, 1973, p. 434; Rubinstein, 1967, pp. 30 –31

[113] Rieff, 1961, p. 29

[114] Freud, 1915/1963c, p. 106

[115] Rieff, 1961, p. 29

[116] Fromm quoted in Greenberg & Mitchell, 1983, p. 110

[117] Yankelovich & Barrett, 1970, p. 29

[118] Jacoby, 1983, p. 102, the language here is Jacoby's

[119] as can be seen from his letters, quoted by Jacoby, 1983, pp. 98 −117

[120] Fenichel, 1938/1954, pp. 89 −109

[121] 1954, p. 287

[122] Borneman, 1976, p. 46

[123] Fenichel, 1938/1954, p. 89

[124] See, Freud, 1915, p. 214 for a clear statement

[125] Freud, 1941, p. 70

[126] see, Laplanche & Pontalis, 1973, pp. 21 −24, 273−276 for references

[127] Fenichel, 1938/1954, p. 90n; Freud, 1917, p. 407

[128] though not as far as Borneman, 1976, pp. 44−70, who goes to the extreme of social reductionism

[129] Fenichel, 1954, p. 90; Fenichel does not actually spell out this dilemma, but it can be extracted from his essay

[130] See., e.g., the concluding pages of Freud, 1904; see., also, Fenichel, 1945, p. 581; Hartmann, 1964, pp. 1−18

[131] Briehi, 1977, p. 74

[132] Springborg, 1981, p. 178

[133] Freud, 1941, p. 70

[134] Marks, 1986, p. 8

[135] see, also, Hampshire, 1960, p. 176

[136] Irani, 1978, p. 7

[137] Marks, 1986, p. 4

[138] Irani, 1978, p. 7

[139] Irani, 1978, p. 8

[140] Hampshire, 1960, p. 176

[141] Freud, 1926, pp. 144 −145;see, Laplanche & Pontalis, 1973, p. 378

[142] Adler, 1959, pp. 1−15; Adler, 1964a, pp. 55−56

[143] See, e.g., Adler, 1964b; Adler, 1964c

[144] see., Reich, 1972a, pp. 18, 54−55; Reich, 1972b, p. 169,n1

[145] Adler, 1907

[146] Fenichel, 1938/1954, p. 95; Fenichel, 1945, p. 40)

[147] Fenichel, 1938/1954, p. 95

[148] Fenichel, 1938/1954, p. 91; like the English word, the various German words for 'power' carry the connotation of efficacy and mastery

[149] Rado, 1926, pp. 396 −413

[150] Rado, 1926, pp. 396 −413more on Abraham shortly

[151] Fenichel, 1954, p. 96

[152] Fenichel, 1938/1954, p. 97

[153] Fenichel was influenced here by Freud, 1923; cf., Fenichel, 1945, pp. 36, 261, 419

[154] Fenichel, 1938/1954, p. 97

[155] Fenichel, 1938/1954, p. 99

[156] Fenichel, 1938/1954, p. 99; one hastens to add, so as not to be accused of an anachronism, that Fenichel was far from being a feminist cf., Fenichel, 1945, pp. 67, 335

[157] Abraham, 1924, pp. 454 −461

[158] Freud, 1917, p. 428; Abraham, 1924, p. 461.

[159] See, Freud, 1923/1960, pp. 18 −20 for more on introjection and objects

[160] Fenichel, 1938/1954, pp. 99 −100

[161] Fenichel, 1938/1954, p. 101

[162] Fenichel, 1938/1954, p. 102

[163] Fenichel, 1938/1954, p. 104 n20

[164] Fenichel, 1938/1954, pp. 106 −107

[165] Jacoby, 1983, pp. 105, 109

[166] Reich, 1970, pp. xxiii, 25

[167] 1983, pp. 173 −183; Gabriel, 1983, p. 182

[168] 1933/1972b, pp. 152 −168

[169] Schneider, 1975, pp. 47 −56

[170] Reich, 1972a, p. 42 n44

[171] Reich, 1972a, pp. 43 −46

[172] Reich, 1972a, pp. 27 −30

[173] see., Benhabib, 1986 for a good summary; also, Schneider, 1975, pp. 213 how 124 relates directly to pleonexia

[174] Fenichel, 1938/1954, p. 92, emphasis in original

[175] Reich, 1972a, p. xix

[176] Cohen, 1982, p. 140

[177] Reich, 1933/1972b, p. xxv

[178] see, Sayers, Evans, & Redclift, 1987; cf., also, Spiro, 1982

[179] Reich, 1933/1972b, p. 163; cf., Chodorow, 1978

[180] Kovel, 1984, p. 107; Kovel's very different views of this process will be examined at the end of this chapter

[181] Cohen, 1982, p. 146; this contrast between Reich and Freud can be seen in their very different views of the superego—in Reich's case as "a foreign body taken from the threatening and prohibiting outer world" and for Freud "as the representative of the internal world of the id"— quoted in Chassequet-Smirgel & Grunberger, 1986, p. 139

[182] compare Freud, 1914, pp. 53, 101 with Reich, 1972a, p. 20n28; Reich, 1933/1972b, p. xxiv;

[183] Reich, 1933/1972b, p. xxvi

[184] Reich, 1933/1972b, especially, pp. 152−281

[185] Reich, 1933/1972b, p. 155

[186] Reich, 1933/1972b, p. 157

[187] Reich, 1933/1972b, p. 174, emphasis in original

[188] Reich, 1933/1972b, pp. 187 −192,09−217

[189] Reich, 1933/1972b, p. 188

[190] Reich, 1933/1972b, p. 188

[191] i.e., to become hardened — Reich, 1933/1972b, p. 189

[192] Reich, 1933/1972b, p. 210 −217, emphasis in original; cf. next, pp.221−224

[193] Reich, 1942/1970, pp.321−322

[194] Abraham, 1917/1948, pp. 299 −302

[195] Abraham, 1921/1948, p. 383

[196] Abraham, 1924/1948, p. 395

[197] Abraham, 1924/1948, p. 423

[198] Abraham, 1917/1948, p. 300

[199] Abraham, 1908/1948, p. 88

[200] Abraham, 1908/1948, pp. 80−89

[201] Schneider, 1975, pp.219 −225

[202] Abraham, 1924/1948, pp. 393 −406

[203] Abraham, 1924/1948, pp. 398 −399

[204] Schneider, 1975, pp. 219 −244

[205] Schneider, 1975, p. 220

[206] 1973, p. 288

[207] in Borneman, 1976, pp. 227 5+2

[208] Borneman, 1976, pp. 237 −242

[209] an observation confirmed by Abraham, 1917/1948, p. 300, and a motive also present in the alcoholic

[210] Borneman, 1976, pp. 237 −238

[211] Borneman, 1976, p. 238

[212] Adams, 1978, pp. 6−7

[213] Chelton & Bonney, 1987, p. 40; pp.40 −47

[214] Chelton & Bonney, 1987, p. 40

[215] Chelton & Bonney, 1987, p. 42

[216] Chelton & Bonney, 1987, p. 42

[217] Chelton & Bonney, 1987, p. 43)

[218] Chelton & Bonney, 1987, pp. 44 −45

[219] Chelton & Bonney, 1987, p. 45

[220] Chelton & Bonney, 1987, p. 45)

[221] Rothstein, 1980, p. 99

[222] Rothstein, 1980, pp. 43 −69

[223] see, Kohut, 1977, p. 193

[224] Kohut, 1971, p. 51

[225] Kohut, 1971, p. 46

[226] Kohut, 1977, pp. 80 −81

[227] Kovel, 1981, p. 27

[228] Kovel, 1981, p. 34; cf., MacIntyre, 1984, esp. pp. 23−35, 181−203

[229] Kovel, 1981, p. 61

[230] Kovel, 1981, p. 66, emphasis in original

[231] Kovel, 1981, p. 70

[232] Kovel, 1981, p. 216

[233] Kovel, 1981, p. 200, emphasis in original

[234] Kovel, 1981, p. 234, emphasis in original

[235] see also., Kovel, 1984 for more on this

[236] Krueger, 1988, p. 574

[237] Krueger, 1988, p. 580

[238] Winsberg, et al., 1999; Landau, et al., 2011; Nedelisky & Steele, 2009

Conclusion

[1] Peterson & Selgman, 2004

[2] Flew, 1956, p.168

[3] for perhaps the clearest expression of these ideas, see Freud, 1920, pp.3–64

[4] see Blumenfield, 1972, for more on this latter point

[5] Krueger, 1982; Winestine, 1985

[6] cf., e.g., Roberts, 2011; Kasser & Kanner, 2002

[7] Kerrin, Hartley, & Rudelius, 2015; Workman & Paper, 2011

[8] 1984, pp.77–94

[9] 1988, p.xiii; Rook, 1987, p.196

[10] Krueger, 1988, p.574; Rook, 1987

[11] 1988, pp.178–179

[12] Winestine, 1988 gave good examples of such fantasies

[13] Rook, 1987, pp.194–195

[14] 1986, p.154

[15] see, for example, Roberts, 2011, pp.146–147 for a summary

[16] Baudrillard, 1998, p.95

[17] Freud, 1914; and later developed by Rothstein, 1980 and Chassequet-Smirgel, 1985, among others

[18] 1986, pp.52–59

[19] Horney, 1937, p. 185

[20] 1976, p.237

[21] e.g., Bursten, 1986, pp.394–395

[22] Laplanche & Pontalis, 1973, p.230; see the discussion of Fenichel and Abraham above

[23] 1986, p. 428

[24] Abraham, 1924, p.454

[25] American Psychiatric Association, p.217

[26] Ghaemi, Stoll, & Pope, 1995

[27] p.10; Kubie, 1971, provides a similar "process" view of mental illness

[28] quoted in Rochberg-Halton, 1986, p138, emphasis in original

[29] 2011, pp.234–236
[30] for a valuable critique of such sociobiological reductionism, see Sahlins, 1978
[31] Kravetz, 1987, p.55
[32] 1981, pp.205–214
[33] quoted in Longres 7 McLeod, 1980, p.267; see also, Kirsh, 1974; Kravetz, 1987
[34] see, e.g., Buber, 1965, pp.1–39
[35] See Freire, 1970 for the classic statement of this position; also, Longres & McLeod, 1980; Berger, 1974 offers possible dangers in Freire's approach
[36] Hartman, 1987
[37] quoted in Herman, 1976, p.100
[38] see, e.g., Peele, 1988, p. xiii
[39] Schafer, 1983, pp. 158–160
[40] see, e.g., Rein, 1970, p. 18; Brodsky, 1976, p. 376 notes this benefit from CR groups
[41] Bergner et al., 1985, p.27
[42] Greenspan, 1988, p.233
[43] Peele, 1988, p.178
[44] for the scientific results, see the articles in Aspinwell & Staudinger, 2003
[45] Stern, 1985, p.123
[46] see Rosengren, 2009; Wagner & Ingersoll, 2013
[47] Kuyken, Padesky, & Dudley, 2011

References

Aboujaoude, E. and L.M. Koran (eds.). *Impulse control disorders.* Cambridge: Cambridge University Press, 2010.

Abraham, K., *Selected papers on psychoanalysis.* London: Hogarth Press, 1948.

Adams, J.W. *Psychoanalysis of drug dependence.* New York: Grune & Stratton, 1978.

Adler, A. *Study of organic inferiority and its psychical compensation.* Translated by R. Jelliffe. New York: Nervous and Mental Disease Publishers.

———. *Individual psychology.* Patterson: littlefield Adams, 1959.

——— *Social Interest: a challenge to mankind.* New York: Capricon, 1964a.

——— *Superiority and social interest.* Evanston: Northwestern University Press, 1964b.

Ainslie, G. "Hyperbolic discounting," In G. Loewenstein and J. Elster (eds.), *Choice over time.,* New York: Russell Sage, (1992), 59–92.

——— "Self-control," In Lowenstein, *Ibid.,* 177–209.

———*Breakdown of will.* New York: Cambridge University Press, 2001.

———."Microeconomic self." In Elster, *The Multiple Self.* Cambridge: Cambridge University Press, (1987), 133–176.

American Psychiatric Association. *Diagnostic and statistical manual of mental disorders,* 3rd ed., revised, Washington, DC: American Psychiatric Press, 1987.

———. *Diagnostic and statistical manual of mental disorders,* 5th ed., Washington, DC: American Psychiatric Press, 2013.

Arendt, H. *The human condition: a study of the central dilemmas facing modern man,* New York: Doubleday Anchor Books, 1959.

Ariely, D. *Predictably irrational: the hidden forces that shape our decisions.* Revised Edition, New York: Harper Collins, 2009.

Arnold, M.B. *Emotion and personality,* Vol.1, New York: Columbia University Press, 1960.

Aspinwell, L.G., U.M. Staudinger. *A psychology of human strengths: fundamental questions and future directions for a positive psychology.* Washington, DC: American Psychological Association Books, 2003.

Balot, R.k. *Greed and injustice in classical Greece.* Princeton: Princeton University Press, 2001

Barber, B. *Consumed: how markets corrupt children, infantile adults, and swallow citizens whole.* New York: W.W. Norton, 2007.

Barthel, D. *Putting on appearances: gender and advertising,* Philadelphia: Temple University Press, 1988.

Baudrillard, J. *Le Systeme des objects:* la *consummation des signe.* Paris: Denoel, 1968.

———*The consumer society: myths and structures,* London: Sage Publications, 1998.

—— *For a critique of the political economy of the sign.* St. Louis, Mo.: Telos Press, 1981.

——*"Au delá du vrai et du faux, ou le malin genie de l'image."* In *Cahiers internationaux de sociologie* (1987), 34,139–145.

Baumeister, R. and K. Vohs (eds.) *The handbook of self-regulation.* New York: Guilfford, 2004.

——,T.F. Heatherton, and D.M. Tice. *Losing control: how people fail at self-regulation.* San Diego, CA: Academic Press, 1994.

Bay, C. *The structure of freedom.* Stanford: Stanford University Press, 1968.

Beatty, S.E. and M.E. Ferrell. "Impulse buying: modeling its precursors," *Journal of Retailing,* (1998), 74, no.2, 169–191.

Beggan, J.K. "On the social nature of nonsocial perception: the more ownership effect," *Journal of Personality and Social Psychology,* (1992), Vol.62, 229–237.

Belenky, M.F., Clinchy, B.M., Goldberger, N.R., & Tarule, J.M. *Women's ways of knowing.* New York: Basic Books, 1986.

Belk, R.W. "Collecting as luxury consumption: effects on individuals and households," *Journal of Economic Psychology,* (1995), 16, no.3, 477–490.

Bellah, R. et al. *The good society.* New York: Alfred A. Knopf, 1992.

Bellegarde, J.D and, M.N. Potenza. "Neurobiology of gambling," In Ross, D., H. Kincaid, and D. Spurrett, (eds.), *What is addiction?* Boston: MIT Press, (2010), 27–51.

Benhabib, S. *Critique, Norm and Utopia.* New York: Columbia University Press, 1986.

——. *Situating the self: gender, community, and postmodernism in contemporary ethics.* New York: Routledge, 1992.

Benson, A.L. (ed.). *I shop, therefore I am: compulsive buying and the search for self.* Northvale, N.J.: Jason Aronson, 2000.

—— and, M. Gengler. "Treating compulsive buying," In R. Coombs, editor, *Handbook of addictive disorders.* (2004), New York: Wiley & Sons, 451–491.

Berger, P.L. "Consciousness raising —to whom? By whom?" *Social Policy,* 5, no.3, (1974): 38–42.

Bergler, E. *Money and emotional conflicts.* New York: International Universities Press, 1959.

Bergner, M., Remer, P., & Whetsell, C. "Transforming women's body image: a feminist counseling approach." *Women and Therapy,* 4, no.3, (1985): 25–38.

Berofsky, B. *Liberation from self: a theory of personal autonomy,* Cambridge: Cambridge University Press, 1995.

Betteridge, H.T. ed. *The New Cassell's German Dictionary.* New York: Funk & Wagnalls, 1965.

Bettleheim, B. *Freud and man's soul.* New York: Alfred Knopf.

Binswanger, L. *Being in the world: selected papers.* New York: Harper & Row, 1968.

Black, D.W. "A review of compulsive buying disorder," *World Psychiatry,* (2007), 6, no.1, 14–18.

——. "Compulsive buying disorder: definition, assessment, epidemiology and clinical management," *CNS Drugs,* (2001), 15, no.1, 17–27.

263

——. "Compulsive buying: clinical aspects," In E. Aboujaoude & L.M. Koran, *Impulse control disorders,* Cambridge: Cambridge University Press, (2010), 5–22.

Bleuler, E. *Textbook of psychiatry.* New York: MacMillan, 1924.

Blumenfield, D. "Free action and unconscious motivation." *Monist,* 56, 426–443.

Boden, M. *Purposive explanation in psychology.* Sussex: Harvester Press, 1978.

Bordo, S. "Anorexia nervosa: psychopathology as a crystallization of culture." *Philosophical Forum,* 17, no.2 (1985–1986): 73–104.

Borgmann, A. *Technology and the character of contemporary life: a philosophical inquiry.* Chicago: University of Chicago Press, 1984.

Borneman, E. (ed.). *The psychoanalysis of money.* New York: Urizen Press, 1976.

Boundy, D. *When money is the drug: the compulsion for credit, cash and chronic debt.* San Francisco: Harper, 1993.

Bratiotis, C. and C.S. Schmalisch *The hoarding handbook: a guide for human service professionals.* New York: Oxford University Press, 2011.

Braun, O.L.and R.A. Wicklund. "Psychological antecedents of conspicuous consumption," *Journal of Economic Psychology,* (1989), 10, no.2, 161–187.

Briehl, W. "Character analysis." In Vol. 3, *International encyclopedia of psychiatry, psychology, psychoanalysis & neurology,* New York: Van Nostrand Reinhold, (1977), 73–76.

Brodsky, A.M. "The consciousness-raising group as a model for therapy with women." In *Female psychology: the emerging self.* Edited by S. Cox. Chicago: Science Research Associates. (1976), 82–94.

Brody, C.M. *Women's therapy groups: paradigms of feminist treatment.* New York: Springer, 1987.

Bruch, H. *Eating disorders: obesity, anorexia nervosa and the person within.* New York: Basic Books, 1973.

Buber, M. *Between man and man.* New York: MacMillan (original published in 1947).

Bursten, B. "Some narcissistic personality types." In *Essential papers on narcissism.* Edited by A.P. Morrison, New York: New York University Press, 1986.

Campbell, C. *The romantic ethic and the spirit of modern consumerism.* Oxford: Basil Blackwell, 1987.

——, "Re-examining Mills on motive: a character vocabulary approach," (1991), *Sociological Analysis,* Vol.52, 89–98

——, "Conspicuous consumption? A critique of Veblen's theory of conspicuous consumption," (1995), 13, no.1, 37–47.

Carver, C and M.F. Scheier. *Attention and self-regulation: a control theory approach to human behavior.* New York: Springer-Verlag, 1981.

Caspary, W.R. *Dewey on democracy.* Ithaca: Cornell University Press, 2000.

Catalano, E.M. and N. Sonenberg. *Consuming passions: help for compulsive shoppers.* Oakland, Ca: New Harbinger, 1993.

Chassequet-Smirgel, J. & B. Grunberger. *Freud or Reich.* London: Free Association Books, 1985.

Chelton, L.G & W. Bonney. "Addiction, affects, and self-object theory." *Psychotherapy,* (1987), 24, no.1, 40–46.

Chodorow, N. *The reproduction of mothering: psychoanalysis and the sociology of gender.* Berkeley: University of California Press, 1978.

Christenson, G.A. et al. "Compulsive buying: descriptive characteristics and psychiatric comorbidity," *Journal of Clinical Psychiatry,* (1994), 55, no.1, 5–11.

—— and S.J. Crow. "The characterization and treatment of trichotillomania," *Journal of Clinical Psychiatry,* (1996), Vol.57, 42–49.

Claes, L. et al. "Emotional reactivity and self-regulation in compulsive buying," *Personality and Individual Differences,* (2010), Vol.49, 526–530.

Clark, A.N., Mankikar, G.D., and I. Gray. "Diogenes syndrome: a clinical study of gross neglect in old age," *Lancet,* (1975), 15, no.1, 366–368.

Clement, C.D. "Misusing psychiatric models: the culture of narcissism." *The Psychoanalytic Review,* (1982), 69, no.2, 283–295.

Coblentz, S.A. *Avarice: a history.* Washington, D.C.: Public Affairs, 1965.

Cohen, I.H. *Ideology and unconsciousness.* New York: New York University Press, 1982.

266

Coles, M.E., et al. "Hoarding behaviors in a large college sample,"
    Behaviour Research and Therapy, (2003), Vol.41, 179–194.

Conrad, P. "Medicalization and social control," *Annual Review of
    Sociology,* (1992), Vol. 18, 209–232.

Cryder, C. et al. "Misery is not miserly: sad and self-focused
    individuals spend more," *Psychological Science,* 19, no.6,
    525–530.

Csikszentmihalyi, M. and E. Rochberg-Halton. *The meaning of things:
    domestic symbols and the self.* Cambridge: Cambridge
    University Press, 1981.

Cushman, P. "Why the self is empty: toward historically situated
    psychology," (1990), 45, no.5, pp.599–611.

——*Constructing the self, constructing America: a cultural history of
    psychotherapy.* New York: Addison-Wiley, 1995.

Dagher, A. "Shopping centers in the brain," *Neuron,*(2007), 53, no.1,
    7–8.

Damasio, A. *Descarte's error: reason and the human brain.* New
    York: Putnam, 1994

——. *The feeling of what happens: body and emotion in the making of
    consciousness.* New York: Harcourt Brace, 1999.

Damon, J.E. *Shopaholics: serious help for addicted spenders.* Los
    Angeles: Price Stein Sloan, 1998

D'Astrous, A. "An enquiry into the compulsive side of "normal"
    consumers," *Journal of Consumer Policy,* (1990), 13, no.1,
    15–31.

Deflem, M. "The sociology of the sociology of money: Simmel and the contemporary battle of the classics," *Journal of Classical Sociology,* (2003), 3, no.1, 67–96.

Delattre, R.A. "The culture of procurement: reflections on addiction and the dynamics of American culture." *Soundings,* (1986), 69, 27–144.

Delphy, C. *Close to home: a materialist analysis of women's oppression.* Amherst: University of Massachusetts, 1984.

Deurzen, E. van. *Psychotherapy and the quest for happiness.* Los Angelas: Sage, 2009

DeSarbo, W.S. and E.A. Edwards. "Typologies of compulsive buying behavior: a constrained clutterwise regression approach," *Journal of Consumer Psychology,* (1996), 5, no.3, 231–262.

Dittmar, H. "A new look at 'compulsive buying': self-discrepancies and materialistic values as predictors of compulsive buying tendency," *Journal of Social and Clinical Psychology,* (2005), 24, no.6, 832–859.

——."Are you what you have? Consumer society and our sense of identity," *Psychologist,* (2004), 17, no.4, 206–210.

——. *The social psychology of material possessions: to have and to be.* New York: St. Martin's Press, 1992.

——. *Consumer culture, identity and well-being.* New York: Psychology Press, 2007.

—— and R. Bond. "I want it and I want it now: using a temporal discounting paradigm to examine predictors of consumer impulsivity," *British Journal of Psychology,* (2010), 101, no.4, 751–776.

Donnelly, M *Managing the mind: a study of medical psychology in early nineteenth century Britain.* London: Tavistock, 1983.

Douglas, M. & B. Isherwood. *The world of goods.* New York: Basic Books, 1979.

Dreyfus, H. "Foucault's therapy." *Psych Critique* (1987), 2, no.1, 65–83.

Durkheim, E. *Suicide: a study in sociology,* New York: Free Press, 1971.

Elliott, R. "Addictive consumption: function and fragmentation in postmodernity," *Journal of Consumer Policy,* (1994), 17, 159–179.

Elster, J. (ed.). *The multiple self.* Cambridge: Cambridge University Press, 1987

—— (ed.). *Addiction: entries and exits.* New York: Russell Sage, 1999.

——and O-J Skog (eds.). *Getting hooked: rationality and addiction.* Cambridge:Cambridge University Press, 2007.

Ertelt, T.W. et al."Current status of cognitive-behavioral intervention for compulsive buying disorder," *Journal of Contemporary Psychotherapy,* (2009), 39, no.4, 213–220.

Ewen, S. *Captains of consciousness: advertising and the social roots of consumer culture.* New York: McGraw Hill, 1976.

——. & E. Ewen. *Channels of desire: mass images and the shaping of American consciousness.* New York: McGraw Hill, 1982.

—— *All consuming images: the politics of style in contemporary culture.* New York: Basic Books, 1988.

Faber, R.J. and T.C. O'Guinn, "Compulsive consumption and credit abuse," *Journal of Consumer Policy,* (1988), 11, no.1, 97–109.

——. "Compulsive buying: a phenomenological exploration," *Journal of Consumer Research,* (1989), 16, no.2, 147–157.

——. "Classifying compulsive consumers: advances in the development of a diagnostic tool," *Advances in Consumer Research,* (1989), Vol.16, 738–744.

——. "A clinical screener for compulsive buying," *Journal of Consumer Research,* (1992), 19, no.3, 459–469.

—— G. Christenson, M. DeZwaan, & J. Mitchell. "Two forms of compulsive consumption: comorbidity of compulsive buying and binge eating," *Journal of Consumer Research,* (1995), 22, no.3, 296–304.

——. *"The urge to buy: a uses and gratifications perspective,"* In S. Ratneshwar, D.G. Mick and C. Huffman (eds.), *The why of consumption: contemporary perspectives on consumer motives, goal, and desires.* London: Routledge, (2000), 177–196.

—— and K.D. Vohs. "To buy or not to buy: self-regulatory failure in purchase behavior," In Baumeister, R. & K. Vohs (eds.) *The handbook of self-regulation.* New York: Guilford, (2004), 509–524.

Fancher, R.T. *Cultures of healing: correcting the image of American healthcare.* San Francisco: W.H. Freeman, 1998

Farb, P. & G. Amelagos. *Consuming passions: the anthropology of eating.* Boston: Houghton Mifflin, 1980.

Fenichel, O. *The psychoanalytic theory of neurosis.* New York: W.W. Norton, 1945.

—— *The collected papers of Otto Fenichel.* 2nd. series. New York: W.W. Norton, 1954.

Ferenczi, S. "Autoplastic and alloplastic adaptation." In M. Balint, ed. *Final contributions to the problems and methods of psychoanalysis.* New York: Brunner Mazel, 1955.

Fingaette, H. *Heavy drinking: the myth of alcoholism as a disease.* Berkeley: University of California Press, 1988.

Fitch, K.E. "Information processing deficits in nonclinical compulsive hoarding," electronic thesis, treatises and dissertations, (2011),paper 4448, Florida State University.

Fitzgerald, R. *Human needs and politics,* Sydney: Pergamon Press, 1977.

—— "Human needs and politics: the ideas of Christian Bay and Herbert Marcuse," *Political Psychology,* (1985), 6, no.1, 87–106.

Flew, A. "Psychoanalytic explanation." *Analysis,* 10, 8–15. Reprinted in M. MacDonald, ed. *Philosophy and analysis.* Oxford: Blackwell, 1956.

—— "Motives and the unconscious." In H. Feigl & M. Scriven, eds. *Minnesota studies in the philosophy of science.* 153–173, Vol. 1. Minneapolis: University of Minnesota, 1956.

Formenek, R. "Learning the lines: women's aging and self esteem." In J.L. Alpert, ed. *Psychoanalysis and women: contemporary reappraisals,* 139–160. Hillsdale: Analytic Press, 1986.

Foucault, M. *Madness and civilization: a history of insanity in the age of reason,* London: Routledge, 2009.

Fox, R.W., & T.J. Lears. *The culture of consumption.* New York: Pantheon, 1983.

Frankfurt, H. *The importance of what we care about: philosophical essays.* Cambridge: Cambridge University Press, 1988.

Freire, P. *Pedagogy of the oppressed.* Translated by M.R. Ramos. New York: Seabury Press, 1971.

Frenkel-Brunswik, E. "Psychoanalysis and the unity of science." *Proceedings of the American Academy of Sciences.* (1954), 80, 271–320.

Freud, A. *The ego and the mechanisms of defense.* Revised edition. New York: International Universities Press, 1946.

Freud, S. "Further recommendations in the technique of psychoanalysis." In S. Freud, *Therapy and Techniques.* 135–156, New York: Collier Books, 1913.

—— *The origins of psychoanalysis.* New York: Basic Books, 1954.

—— *The ego and the id.* New York: W.W. Norton, 1960.

—— *Beyond the pleasure principle.* New York: W.W. Norton, 1961.

——Civilization *and its discontents.* New York: W.W. Norton, 1962.

——*Early psychoanalytic writings.* New York: Collier, 1963a.

——*Therapy and technique.* New York: Collier, 1963b.

——*General psychological theory.* New York: Collier, 1963c.

——*Sexuality and the psychology of love.* New York: Collier, 1963d.

——*The problem of anxiety.* New York: W.W. Norton, 1963e.

——*The psychopathology of everyday life.* New York: W.W. Norton, 1965.

——*Freud and Breuer: studies on hysteria.* New York: Avon, 1966a.

——*Introductory lectures on psychoanalysis.* New York: W.W. Norton, 1966b.

——*History of the psychoanalytic movement.* New York: Collier, 1967.

——*Character and culture.* New York: Collier, 1968a.

——*The sexual enlightenment of children.* New York: Collier, 1968b.

——*New introductory lectures.* New York: W.W. Norton, 1968c.

——*An outline of psychoanalysis.* New York: W.W. Norton, 1969.

Fromm, E. "The psychological aspects of the guaranteed income." In R. Theobald, ed., *The Guaranteed income: next step in economic evolution.* 175–184, New York: Doubleday, 1964.

—— *To have or to be?* London: Bloomsbury Academic, 2014.

Frost, R. & G. Steketee. *Stuff: compulsive hoarding and the meaning of things.* Boston: Houghton Mifflin, 2010.

—— & Steketee. *The Oxford handbook of hoarding and acquiring.* New York: Oxford University Press, 2014.

——G. Steketee, and L. Williams. "Compulsive buying, compulsive hoarding, and obsessive-compulsive disorder," *Behaviour Research & Therapy,* (2002), Vol.33, 201–213.

——, M. Kyrios, K.D. McCarthy, & Y. Mathews. "Self-ambivalence and attachment to possessions," *Journal of Cognitive Psychotherapy,* (2007), Vol.21, 232–242.

——,G. Steketee, and J. Grisham. "Measurement of compulsive hoarding: saving inventory—revised," *Behavioral Research and Therapy,* (2004), Vol.42, 1163–1182.

——,G. Steketee, and L. Williams. "Hoarding: a community health problem," *Health and Social Care in the Community,* (2000), Vol.8, 229–234.

——, G. Patronek, and E. Rosenfield. "Comparison of object and animal hoarding," *Depression and Anxiety,* (2011), Vol.28, 885–891.

—— and T.L. Hartl. "A cognitive-behavioral model of compulsive hoarding," *Behaviour Research and Therapy,* (1996), Vol.34, 341–350.

——et al. "Hoarding, compulsive buying, and reasons for saving," *Behaviour Research and Therapy,* (1998), 39, no.7, 657–664.

——P. Marten, C. Lahart, and R. Rosenblate. "The dimensions of perfectionism," *Cognitive Therapy and Research,* (1990), 14, no.5, 449–468.

——et al. "Motives for acquiring and saving in hoarding disorder, OCD and community controls," *Journal of Obsessive-Compulsive and Related Disorders,* (2014), Vol.4, 54–59.

——, D.F. Tolin and N. Maltby. "Insight-related challenges in the treatment of hoarding," *Cognitive and Behavioral Practice,* (2010), 17, no.4, 404–413.

Gabriel, Y. *Freud and society.* London: Routledge & Keegan Paul, 1983.

Galbraith, J.K. *The affluent society.* Boston: Houghton Mifflin, 1958.

—— *The good society: the human agenda.* Boston: Houghton Mifflin, 1996.

Gardner, M.P. "Mood states and consumer behavior: a critical review," *Journal of Consumer Research,* (1985), 12, no.3, 281–300.

Garfinkel, P.E. & D.M. Garner. *Anorexia nervosa: a multidimensional perspective.* New York: Brunner Mazel, 1982.

Germain, C. B. & A. Gitterman. *The life model of social work practice.* New York: Columbia University Press, 1980.

Ghaemi, S.N., A.L. Stoll and H.G. Pope, Jr. "Lack of insight in bipolar disorder: the acute manic episode," *Jounal of Nervous and Mental Disease,* (1995), 183, no.3, 464–467.

Gilbert, D.T, M.J. Gill, and T.D. Wilson. "The future is now: temporal correction in affective forecasting," *Organizational Behavior and Human Decision Processes.* (2002), 88, no.1, 430–444.

Giovanni, Z., et al. "Diogenes syndrome or isolated syllogomania? Four heterogeneous clinical cases," *Aging Clinical Experimental Research,* (2013), 25, no.4, 473–478.

Gjelsvik, O. "Freedom of will and addiction," In J. Elster (ed.), *Addiction: entries and exits,* 29–54.

Glatt, M.M. and C.C.H. Cook. "Pathological spending as a form of psychological dependence," *British Journal of Addiction,* (1987), 82, no.11, 1257–1258.

Goldberg, H. & R. Lewis. *Two patterns of rationality in Freud's writings.* Tuscaloosa: University of Alabama, 1988.

Goldman, R. "When buying is an addiction," In A.L. Benson, (ed.) *I shop, therefore I am.* (2000), 245–267.

Graaf, J. de, D. Wann, and T. Naylor, *Affluenza: the all-consuming epidemic.* San Francisco: Berrett-Koehler, 2001.

Grant, J.E., M.N. Potenza, A. Weinstein, & D. Gorelick, "Introduction to behavioral addictions," *Alcohol Abuse,* (2010), 36, no.5, 233–241.

Greenberg, J.R. & S.A. Mitchell. *Object relations in psychoanalytic theory.* Cambridge: Harvard University Press, 1983.

Greenblatt, S. *Renaissance self-fashioning: from More to Shakespeare.* Chicago: Chicago University Press, 1980.

Greenspan, M. *A new approach to women and therapy.* New York: McGraw-Hill, 1983.

Grisham, J.R. "Compulsive hoarding: current controversies and new directions," *Dialogues in Clinical Neuroscience,* (2010), 12, no.2, 233–240.

Grünbaum, A. *The foundations of psychoanalysis.* Berkeley: University of California Press, 1984.

Hadot, P. *Philosophy as a way of life,* Malden, MA: Blackwell, 1995.

Hampshire, S. "Disposition and memory." *International Journal of psychoanalysis.* (1960), 43, no.1. 59–68.

——. "Dispositions," In S. Hampshire, *Freedom of mind: and other essays by Stuart Hampshire.* 34–41, Princeton: Princeton University Press, 1971.

Hartman, S. "Therapeutic self-help groups: a process of empowerment for women in abusive relationships." In C.M. Brody, (ed.), *Women's therapy groups: paradigms of feminist treatment.* 67–81, New York: Springer, 1987.

Hartman, H. "Understanding and explanation. In H. Hartman, *Essays on ego psychology: selected problems in psychoanalytic theory.* Translated by J. Needleman. 369–403. New York: Initernational Universities Press, 1954.

Hartsock, N.C.M. *Money, sex, and power.* Boston: Northeastern University Press, 1985.

Hartston, H. "The case for compulsive shopping as an addiction," *Journal of Psychoactive Drugs,* (2012), 44, no.1, 64–67.

Haug, W.F. *Critique of commodity aesthetics: appearance, sexuality and advertising in capitalist society.* Minneapolis: University of Minnesota Press, 1986.

Heath, N. and R.E. Vuchinich, (eds.), *Choice, behavioral economics and addiction.* Burlington: Elsevier, 2003.

Heelas, P. and P. Morris (eds.). *The values of the enterprise culture: the moral debate.* London; Routledge, 1992.

Heilbroner, R. *Marxism: for and against.* 1st. edition, New York: W.W. Norton, 1980.

Hempel, C.G. *Aspects of scientific explanation.* New York: Free Press, 1965.

Herman, R.D. *Gamblers and gambling: methods, institutions, and controls.* Lexington: Lexington Books, 1976.

Hirschman, A.O. *The passions and the interests: political arguments for capitalism before its triumph.* Princeton: Princeton University Press, 1977.

—— *Shifting involvements: private interest and public action.* 20th anniversary edition, Princeton: Princeton University Press, 2002.

Hirschman, E.C. "The consciousness of addiction: toward a general theory of compulsive consumption," *Journal of Consumer Research,* (1992), 19, no.2, 155–179.

Hoch, S.J. and G. Loewenstein. "Time-inconsistent preferences and consumer self-control," *Journal of Consumer research,* (1991), Vol.17, 492–507.

Hollander, E. and A. Allen. "Is compulsive buying a real disorder and is it really compulsive?" *American Journal of Psychiatry,* (2006), 163, no10, 1670–1672.

Horney, K. *The neurotic personality of our time.* New York: W.W. Norton, 1964.

Horowitz, D. *The morality of spending.* Baltimore: Johns Hopkins University Press, 1985.

Ignatieff, M. *The needs of strangers.* New York: Picador USA, 1984.

Illouz, E. *Consuming the romantic utopia: love and the cultural contradictions of capitalism.* Berkeley: University of California Press, 1997.

Ingham, G.R. *Pleonexia: a modern pathology of self.* Masters Thesis. Smith College for Social Work, 1989.

Irani, K.D. "Explanation in psychoanalytic theory." In K.D. Irani, L.Horowitz & G. Myers (eds.), New York: Haven Press, 1978.

"Is the consumer-credit society running out of control?" *Economist.* 71–75, April 6, 1985.

Izenberg, G.N. *The existential critique of Freud.* Princeton: Princeton University Press, 1976.

Jacoby, R. *Social amnesia: a critique of contemporary psychology from Adler to Lang.* New York: Beacon Press, 1975.

—— "Narcissism and the spirit of capitalism." *Telos,* Vol.44, 58–74.

—— *The repression of psychoanalysis: Otto Fenichel and the political Freudians.* New York: Basic Books, 1983.

Jaeger, W. *Paedeia: the ideals of Greek culture.* Vols. 1 & 3. New York: Oxford University Press, 1944.

Jones, E. *The life and work of Sigmund Freud.* 3 Volumes. New York: Basic Books, 1953.

——"The theory of symbolism." In E. Jones, *Papers on psychoanalysis.* 87–144. Boston: Beacon Press, 1961.

Kacen, J.J. and J.A. Lee. "The influence of culture on consumer impulse buying behavior," *Journal of Consumer Psychology,* (2002), 12, no.2, 163–176.

Kahneman, D. *Thinking fast and slow.* New York: Farrar, Straus and Giroux, 2011.

——, A. Tversky (eds.). *Choices, values and frames.* New York: Cambridge University Press, 2000.

——, D. Diener, and N. Schwartz, (eds.). *Well-being: the foundations of hedonic psychology.* New York: Russell Sage, 1999.

——, J.L. Knetsch, and R.H. Thaler. "Experimental tests of the endowment effect and the Coase theorem," *Journal of Political Economy,* (1990), 98, no.6, 1325–1348.

Kasser, T. and A.D. Kanner (eds.) *Psychology and consumer culture: the struggle for a good life in a materialistic world.* Washington, D.C.: APA, 2004.

Kasser, T. *The high price of materialism.* Cambridge, MA: MIT Press, 2002.

Kaufman, W. "Some emotional uses of money." In E. Borneman (ed.), *The Psychoanalysis of money.* 227–251. New York: Urizon Books, 1976.

Keynes, J.M. *Essays in biography.* New York: W.W. Norton, 1951.

Keefe, T. "Alienation and social work practice." *Social Casework,* Vol. 56, no.3, 145–153.

Keinan, A. and R. Kivetz. "Remedying hyperopia: the effects of self-control on consumer behavior," *Journal of Marketing Research,* (2008), Vol. XLV, 676–689.

Kennett, J. *Agency and responsibility: a common-sense moral psychology.* New York: Oxford University Press, 2001.

Kernberg, O. "Problems in the classification of personality disorders." In O. Kernberg, *Severe personality disorders: psychotherapeutic strategies.* 77–94. New Haven: Yale University Press, 1984.

Kerrin, R.A., S.W. Hartley, & W. Rudelius. *Marketing: the core.* 6th edition, Boston: McGraw Hill, 2015.

Keynes, J.M. *Essays in persuasion.* New York: W.W. Norton, 1963.

——, *Essays in biography.* New York: W.W. Norton, 1951.

Khalidi, M.A. "Carving nature at the joints," *Philosophy and Science,* (1993), 60, no.1, 100–113.

Kincaid, H. and J.A. Sullivan. "Medical models of addiction," In D. Ross, et al. (eds.) *What is addiction?* Cambridge, MA: MIT Press, 2010.

King, R. *The party of eros.* Chapel Hill: University of North Carolina, 1972.

Kirsh, B. "Consciousness-raising groups as therapy for women." In V. Franks & V. Burtle (eds.), *Women in therapy: new psychotherapy for a changing society.* 326–354. New York: Brunner Mazel, 1974.

——"The evolution of consciousness-raising groups." In C. Brody (ed.) Women's therapy groups: paradigms of feminist treatment. 43–54. New York: Springer, 1987.

Kivetz, R. and A. Keinan. "Repenting hyperopia: an analysis of self-control regrets," *Journal of Consumer Research,* Vol.33, 273–282.

Kohut, H. *The analysis of the self.* New York: International Universities Press, 1971.

Koran, L.M. et al. "Estimated prevalence of compulsive buying behavior in the United States," *American Journal of Psychiatry,* (2006), 163, no.10, 1806–1812.

Kottler, J.A. *Exploring and treating acquisitive desire: living in the material world.* Thousand Oaks: Sage, 1999.

Kovel, J. *The age of desire.* New York: Pantheon, 1981.

Knutson, B., et al. "Neural antecedents of the endowment effect,"
  Neuron, (2008), 58, no.5, 814–822.

Kraepelin, E. *Psychiatrie: ein lehrbuch für studierende und ärzte.*
  Leipsig: J.A. Barth, 1909.

Kravitz, D. "Benefits of consciousness-raising groups for women." In
  C. Brody, *Women's therapy groups: paradigms of feminist
  treatment.* 55–66. New York: Springer, 1987.

Krueger, D.W. "On compulsive shopping and spending: a
  psychodynamic inquiry." *American Journal of Psychotherapy,*
  (1988), 42, no.4, 574–584.

——. (ed.). *The last taboo: money as symbol and reality in
  psychotherapy and psychoanalysis.* New York: Brunner/Mazel,
  1986.

Kubie, L.S. "Multiple fallacies in the concept of schizophrenia."
  Journal of Nervous and Mental Diseases. (1971), 153, no5,
  331–342.

Kuyken, W., C.A. Padesky, & R. Dudley. *Collaborative case
  conceptualization: working effectively with clients in cognitive-
  behavioral therapy.* New York: Guilford Press, 2011.

Kyrios, M., et al. "Cognitions in compulsive buying and acquisition,"
  Cognitive Therapy and Research, (2004), 28, no.2, 241–258.

Lacan, J. *Speech and language in psychoanalysis.* Baltimore: Johns
  Hopkins University Press, 1968.

Landau, D., et al. "Stressful life events and material deprivation in
  hoarding disorder," *Journal of Anxiety Disorders,* (2011), 25,
  no.2, 192–203.

Laplanche, J. & J.B. Pontalis. *The language of psychoanalysis.* New York: W.W. Norton, 1973.

Lasch, C. *The minimal self: psychic survival in troubled times.* New York: W.W. Norton, 1984.

Layard, A. *Happiness: lessons from a new science.* New York: Penguin Press, 2005.

Lears, J. *Fables of abundance: a cultural history of advertising in America.* New York: Basic Books, 1994.

Lee, S. and A. Mysyk, "The medicalization of compulsive buying," *Social Science & Medicine,* (2004), 58, no.9, 1709–1718.

Lee, S-H, S.J. Lennon, and N.A. Rudd. "Compulsive consumption tendencies among television shoppers," *Family and Consumer Sciences,* (2000), 28, no.4, 463–488.

Leiss, W., S. Kline & S. Jhally (eds.) *Social communication in advertising: persons, products, and images of well-being.* 3rd edition, New York: Routledge, 2005.

—— *The limits of satisfaction: an essay on needs and commodities.* Toronto: University of Toronto, 1976.

Lennon, S.J., M.M. Sanik, and N.F. Stanforth. "Motivation for television shoppers: clothing purchase frequency and personal characteristics," *Clothing and Textile Research Journal,* (2003), 21, no.2, 63–74.

Leonard, P. *Personality and ideology: towards a materialist understanding of the individual.* London: MacMillan, 1984.

Lerman, H. "What happens in feminist therapy." In S. Cox (ed.) *Female psychology: the emerging self.* 378–384. Chicago: Science Research Associates, 1976.

Lessig, L. *Republic lost: how money corrupts Congress and a plan to stop it.* New York: Twelve Book, 2011.

Levy, N. (ed.). *Addiction and self-control: perspectives from philosophy, psychology, and neuroscience.* Oxford: Oxford University Press, 2013.

Lichtman, R. *The production of desire: the integration of psychoanalysis into Marxism.* New York: The Free Press, 1982.

Longres, J.F. & E. McLeod. "Consciousness-raising and social work practice." *Social Casework,* Vol.61, (1980), 267–276.

Loewenstein, G. and J. Elster. (eds.), *Choice over time.* New York: Russell Sage, 1992.

—— "Out of control: visceral influences on behavior," *Organizational Behavior and Decision Processes,* (1996), 65, no.3, 272–292.

—— "The creative destruction of decision research," *Journal of Consumer Research,* (2001), 28, no.3, 499–505.

Lukács, G. *History and class consciousness.* Translated by R. Livingston. Cambridge: M.I.T. Press, 1924.

Lukes, S. *Power: a radical view.* Houndmills, U.K.:MacMillan, 1974.

MacAndrew, C. "On the possibility of an addiction-free mode of being." In S. Peele (ed.), *Visions of addiction: major contemporary perspectives on addiction and alcoholism.* 163–181. Lexington: Lexington Books, 1988.

MacIntyre, A. *The unconscious.* London: Rutledge * Kegan Paul, 1958.

——"Motives and causes." *Proceedings of the Aristotelian Society: Supplement.* (1959), Vol. 19, 139–162.

—— *After virtue: a study in moral theory.* 3rd. edition, London: Bloomsbury Press, 2013.

——*Whose justice? Which rationality?* South Bend: University of Notre Dame Press, 1988.

Maher, R.F. *New men of Papua: a study in culture change.* Madison: University of Wisconsin Press, 1961.

Malhorta, N.K. "Self concept and product choice: an integrated perspective." *Journal of Economic* Psychology, (1988), Vol.9, 1–28.

Marks, J. *The ways of desire.* Chicago: Precedent, 1986.

McAdams, D.P. *The person: an introduction to the science of personality psychology.* 5th edition, New York: Wiley 2009.

McCracken, G.D. *Culture and consumption: new approaches to the symbolic character of consumer goods and activities.* Bloomington, IN: Indiana University Press, 1990.

McCracken, J. *Taste and the household: the domestic ascetic and moral reasoning.* Albany: State University of New York Press, 2001.

McElroy, S.L., et al. "Compulsive buying: a report of 20 cases," *Journal of Clinical Psychiatry,* (1995), 55, no.6, 242–248.

McGrath, W.J. *Freud's discovery of psychoanalysis.* Ithaca: Cornell University Press, 1986.

Meissner, A. "Narcissistic personalities and borderline conditions: a
differential diagnosis." In A. Morrison (ed.), *Essential papers
on narcissism*. 403–437. New York: New York University
Press, 1986.

Mele, A.R. *Self-deception unmasked*. Princeton: Princeton University
Press, 2001.

Messer, S.B., L.A. Sass, & R.L. Woolfolk, (eds.). *Hermeneutics and
psychological theory: interpretive perspectives on personality,
psychotherapy, and psychopathology*. New Bronswick: Rutgers
University Press, 1988.

Messiha, F.S. "Fluoxetine: a spectrum of clinical applications and
postulates of underlying mechanisms," *Neuroscience and
Behavioral Reviews,* (1993), 17, no.4, 385–396.

Mick, D.G. et al. (eds). *Transformative consumer research for
personal and collective well-being*. New York: Routledge,
2012.

Miller, V.J. "Slavery and commodity chains: fighting the globalization
of indifference," *America: the National Catholic Review,* Jan.
2, 2014.

Miller, W.R. and S. Rollnick. *Motivational interviewing: helping
people change*. 3rd. edition, New York: Guilford Press, 2013.

Miltenberger, R.G., et al. "Direct and retrospective assessment of
factors contributing to compulsive buying," *Journal of
Behavioral Therapy and Experimental Psychiatry,* (2003),
34,no.1, 1–9.

Mintz, L.B. & N.E. Betz. "Sex differences in the nature, realism, and correlates of body image." *Sex Roles,* Vol.15, 185–195.

Mischel, W. *The marshmallow test: mastering self-control.* London: Bantam Books, 2014.

Mitchell, J.E. et al, "Cognitive behavioral therapy for compulsive buying disorder," *Behavior Research and Therapy,* (2006), 44, no.12, 1859–1865.

Mitchell, S.A. and L. Aron (eds.). *Relational psychoanalysis: the emergence of a tradition.* Vol.14, New York: Routledge, 1999.

Monahan, P. "Reliability and validity of a scale to measure change in persons with compulsive buying," *Psychiatry Research,* (1996), 64, no.1, 59–67.

Morino, J.A. et al. "Compulsive buying," In B.A. Johnson (ed.), *Addiction medicine: science and practice.* New York: Springer, (2012), 649–660.

Morrison, A. *Essential papers on narcissism.* New York: New York University Press, 1986.

Muller, J.Z. *The mind and the market: capitalism in modern European thought.* New York: Alfred Knopf, 2002.

Müller, A. et al. "Hoarding in a compulsive buying sample," *Behavior Research and Therapy,* (2007), 45, no.1, 2754–2763.

—— et al. "Psychiatric aspects of impulsivity," *American Journal of Psychiatry,* (2001) 158, no.11, 1783–1793.

Müller, A. and J.E. Mitchell. *Compulsive buying: clinical foundations and treatment.* New York: Routledge, 2011.

Muruganantham, G and R.S. Bhaket. "A review of impulsive buying behavior," *International Journal of Marketing Studies*, (2013), 5, no.3, 149.

Nedelisky, A and M. Steele. "Attachment to people and to objects in obsessive-compulsive disorder: an exploratory comparison of hoarders and non-hoarders," *Attachment and Human Development*, (2009), 11, no.4, 365–383.

Neu, J. *Emotion, thought and therapy: a study of Hume and Spinoza and the relationship of philosophical theories of the emotions to psychological theories of therapy.* Berkeley: University of California Press, 1977.

Nordsletten, A.E. and D. Mataix-Cols. "Hoarding versus collecting: where does pathology diverge from play?" *Clinical Pathology Review*, (2012), 32, no.3, 165–176.

North, H. *Sophrosyne: self-knowledge and self-restraint in Greek literature.* Ithaca, N.Y.: Cornell University Press, 1966.

Nussbaum, M.C. *The therapy of desire: theory and practice in Hellenistic ethics.* Princeton: Princeton University Press, 1994.

——.*Upheavals of thought: the intelligence of emotions.* Cambridge: Cambridge University Press, 2001.

——. *Hiding from humanity: disgust, shame, and the law.* Princeton: Princeton University Press, 2004.

O'Connor, J. "To hold on, or to let go? loss and substitution in the process of hoarding," *European Journal of Psychotherapy and Counseling*, (2014), 16, no.2, 101–113.

Oldham, J., E. Hollander, and A. Skodol. *Impulsivity and compulsivity.* Washington, DC: American Psychiatric Press, 1996.

O'Neil, J. "The 'productive body': an essay on the work of consumption." *Queen's Quarterly,* (1978), Vol.85, 221–230.

Orbach, S. *Hunger strike: the anoretic's struggle as a metaphor for our age.* New York: W.W. Norton, 1986.

Pachaska, J.O., J. Norcross, & C.C. Diclemente. *Changing for good: a revolutionary six-stage program for overcoming bad habits and moving your life positively forward.* New York: Collins, 2007.

Patronek, G.J. "Hoarding in animals: an under-recognized public health problem in a difficult to study population," (1999), 114, no1, 81–87.

Peele, St. *Visions of addiction: major contemporary perspectives on addiction and alcoholism.* Lexington: Lexington Books, 1988.

——.with A. Brodsky. *Love and addiction.* New York: Taplinger Publishing, 1975.

Peters, R.S. *The concept of motivation.* London: Routledge & Kegan Paul, 1960.

Peterson, C. and M. Seligman. *Character strengths and virtues.* Washington, DC: American Psychological Association, 2004.

Petry, N.M. and J.G. Madden, "Discounting and pathological gambling," In G.J. Madden & W.K. Bickel, (eds.) *Impulsivity: the behavioral and neurological science of discounting,* Washington, DC: APA Books, 2010.

Poggi, G. *Money and the modern mind: Georg Simmel's philosophy of money.* Berkeley: University of California Press, 1993.

Preteceille, E. & J.P. Ferrail. *Capitalism, consumption and need.* London: Basil Blackwell, 1985.

Rado, S. "The psychic effect of intoxicants." In S. Rado, *Psychoanalysis of behavior.* Vol.1, New York: Grune & Stratton, 1956.

Rapaport, D. *The collected papers of David Rapaport.* Edited by M. Gill. New York: Basic Books, 1967.

Reich, A. "Pathologic forms of self-esteem regulation." In A. Morrison (ed.). *Essential papers on narcissism.* New York: New York University Press, 1986.

Reich, W. *The mass psychology of fascism.* New York: Simon & Schuster, 1970.

——*Sex-pol: essays 1929–1934.* New York: Vintage Books, 1972a.

——*Character analysis.* 3rd edition. New York: Farrar, Strauss & Giroux, 1972b.

Rein, M. "Social work in search of a radical profession." *Social Work,* Vol.15, no.2. (1970), 13–28.

Richards, A.K. "Clothes and the couch," In A.L. Benson (ed.) *I shop, therefore I am.* (2000), 311–337.

Richards, B. *Capitalism and infancy: essays on psychoanalysis and politics.* London: Free Association Books, 1984.

Richins, M.L. and S. Dawson. "A consumer values orientation for materialism and its measurement: scale development and validation," *Journal of Consumer Research,* (1992), 19, no.3, 303–316.

—— "Valuing things: the public and private meanings of possessions," *Journal of Consumer Research,* (1994), 21, no.3, 504–521.

Ricoeur, P. *Freud and philosophy.* New Haven: Yale University Press, 1970.

Rieff, P. *Freud: the mind of the moralist.* New York: Anchor Books, 1961.

——*The triumph of the therapeutic.* New York: Harper & Row, 1966.

Roberts, J.A. *Shiny objects: why we spend money we don't have in search of happiness we can't buy.* New York: Harper Collins, 2012.

——and J.F. Tanner, Jr. "Compulsive buying and risky behavior among adolescents," *Psychological Reports,* (2000), 86, no.3, 736–770.

——and E. Jones. "Money attitudes, credit use, and compulsive buying among American college students," *The Journal of Consumer Affairs,* (2001), 35, no.21, 213–240.

——and S.F. Pirog. "Personal goals and their role in consumer behavior: the case of compulsive buying," *Journal of Marketing Theory and Practice,* (2004), Vol.12, 61–73.

Robertson, A.F. *Greed: gut feelings, growth, and history.* Cambridge: Polity Press, 2001.

Robinson, P.A. *The Freudian left.* New York: Harper & Row, 1969.

Rochberg-Halton, E. *Meaning and modernity: social theory in the pragmatic attitude.* Chicago: University of Chicago Press, 1986.

Rook, D.W. "The buying impulse." *Journal of Consumer Research.* (1987), Vol.14, 189–199.

—— and M.P. Gardner, "In the mood: impulse buying's affective antecedents," In J. Arnold-Costa and R.W. Belk, (eds.) *Research in Consumer Behavior,* (1993), Vol.6, 1–28.

—— and R.J. Fisher. "Normative influences on impulsive buying behavior," *Journal of Consumer Research,* (1995), Vol.22, 305–313.

Rorty, A.O. "Enough already with 'theories of emotions,' In R.C. Solomon, (ed.), *Thinking about feeling: contemporary philosophers on emotions,* 269–278, Oxford: Oxford University Press, 2004.

Rosengren, D.B. *Building motivational interviewing skills: a practitioner workbook.* New York: Guilford Press, 2009.

Ross, D., H. Kincaid, and D. Spurrett, (eds.). *What is addiction?* Boston: MIT Press, 2010.

Rothstein, A. *The narcissistic pursuit of perfection.* New York: International Universities Press, 1984.

Rubinstein, B. "Explanation and mere description: a metascientific examination of certain aspects of psychoanalytic theory of motivation." In M. Gill (ed.) *Motives and thoughts: psychoanalytic essays in honor of David Rapaport.* 20–70. New York: International Universities Press, 1967.

——"On metaphor and related phenomena."In R. Holt & E. Peterfreund (eds.), *Psychoanalysis and contemporary science,* 70–109, Vol.1, New York: MacMillan, 1972.

——"On the logic of explanation in psychoanalysis." In B. Rubinstein (ed.), *Psychoanalysis and contemporary science.* (1973), Vol.2, 338–358. New York: MacMillan.

——"On the role of classification processes in mental functioning: aspects of a psychoanalytic theoretical model." In L. Goldberger & V. Rosen (eds.) (1974), Vol.3, 101–188. New York: MacMillan.

Ruden, R.A. and M. Byalick. *The craving brain: a bold new approach to breaking free from drug addiction, overeating, alcoholism, and gambling.* New York: Harper Collins, 1997.

Saad, G. *The consuming instinct: what juicy burgers, Ferrris, pornography, and gift-giving reveal about human nature.* Amherst, NY: Prometheus Books., 2011.

Sadler, J.Z. *Values and psychiatric diagnosis.* Oxford: oxford University Press, 2005.

Sahlins, M. *The use and abuse of biology: an anthropological critique of sociobiology.* Ann Arbor: University of Michigan Press, 1978.

Samuels, J.F. et al. "Prevalence and correlates of hoarding behavior in a community sample," *Behavior Research & Theory,* (2008), 46, no.7, 836–844.

Sandel, M.J. *What money can't buy: the moral limits of markets.* New York: Farrar, Straus & Giroux, 2012.

Sander, M. "Bibliomania," *Journal of Criminal Law and Criminology,* (1943), 34, no.3, 155–161.

Sandford, L.T. & M.E. Donovan. *Women and self-esteem: understanding and improving the way we think about ourselves and feel about ourselves.* New York: Penguin Books, 1984.

Saxema, S. "Recent advances in compulsive hoarding," *Current Psychiatry Reports,* (2008), 10, no.4, 297–303.

———. "Neurobiology and treatment of compulsive hoarding," *CNS Spectrum,* (2008), 13, no.9, 29–36.

Sayer, J., M. Evans, & N. Redclift (eds.) *Engels revisited: new feminist essays.* London: Tavistock, 1987.

Schacter, S. *Emotion, obesity, and crime.* New York: Academic Press, 1971.

Schafer, R. *A new language of psychoanalysis.* New Haven: Yale University Press, 1976.

———*The analytic attitude.* New York: Basic Books, 1983.

———"Lecture delivered on *The Analytic Attitude* at the meeting of the Psychoanalytic Society, University of Massachusetts, Amherst, 1989.

Scherhorn, G. "The addictive trait in buying behavior," *Journal of Consumer Policy,* (1990), 13, no.1, 33–52.

Schor, J. *Do Americans shop too much?* Boston: Beacon Press, 2000.

Schneider, M. *Neurosis and civilization.* New York: Seabury Press, 1975.

Schosser, S. et al. "Compulsive buying: demography, phenomenology, and comorbidity in 46 subjects," *General Hospital Psychiatry,* (1994), 16, no.3, 205–212.

Scitovsky, T. *The joyless economy: the psychology of human satisfaction,* revised edition, New York: Oxford University Press, 1992.

Sen, A. *Commodities and capabilities.* New York: Elsevier Science, 1985.

Shaffer, H.J. "The most important unresolved issue in addictions: conceptual chaos," *Substance Use and Misuse,* (1997), 32, no.11, 1573–1580.

Shope, R.K. "Freud on conscious and unconscious intentions." 149–159, *Inquiry,* 13, 1970.

——"Freud's concept of meaning." In B. Rubinstein (ed.), *Psychoanalysis and contemporary science.* 276–303, Vol.2, New York: MacMillan, 1973.

——"The significance of Freud for modern philosophy of mind." In G. Gloistad (ed.) *Contemporary philosophy,* 101–122, Vol.4, Boston: Nijhoff, 1985.

Shell, M. *Money, language, and thought.* Berkeley: University of California Press, 1982.

Simmel, G. *Philosophes des geldes* (*Philosophy of money*). Leipsig: Verlogvon Duncer& Humlot, 1907.

——" Das problem des stiles (The problem of styles)." 7, 307–316, *Dekorative Künst,* 11, 1908.

——*Philosophische kultur, über das abenteur, die geschlecter und die krise der modern: gesammelts essays (Philosophical culture: collected essays).* 2nd. edition, Leipsig: Verlag Klaus Wagenbach, 1986.

——*Brücke und tür (Bridge and door).* Stuttgart: K. Fr. Kochler, 1957.

——"Fashion." In G. Simmel, *On individuality and social forms.* 294–323. Chicago: University of Chicago Press, 1971a.

——"The metropolis and mental life." In G. Simmel, *Ibid.* 324–339, 1971b.

——*The philosophy of money.* Boston: Routledge & Kegan Paul, 1978.

Simon, W. "Reflections on the relationship between the individual and society." In W. Simon, *Human futures.* 141–157. London: IPC Science & Technology Press, 1974.

——"The anomie of affluence: a post Mertonian conception." 356–378, *AJS,* 82, no.2, 1976.

Skidelsky, R. *Keynes: the return of the master.* New York: Public Affairs, 2010.

Smith, R.L. *Treatment strategies for substance abuse and process addictions.* Alexandria, VA: American Counseling Association, 2015.

Sohn, H-H. and Y-J. Choi. "A model of compulsive buying: dysfunctional beliefs and self-regulation of compulsive buyers," *Social Behavior and Personality,* (2012), 40, no.10, 1611–1624.

Spencer, S. "Hoarding raises health, safety risks," *Worcester Telegram & Gazette,* Nov. 13, 2013.

Spiro, M. *Oedipus in the Trobriands.* Chicago: University of Chicago Press, 1982.

Steketee, G. and R.O. Frost. *Treatment for hoarding disorder: a therapist guide.* New York: Oxford University Press, 2013.

——. *Treatment for hoarding disorder: workbook.* New York: Oxford University Press, 2013.

Steketee, G., R. Frost, and M. Kyrios. "Cognitive aspects of compulsive hoarding," *Cognitive Therapy and Research,* (2003), 27, no.4, 463–479.

Stern, D. *The interpersonal world of the infant.* New York: Basic Books, 1985.

Stout, J. *Ethics after Babel: the languages of morals and their discontents.* Boston: Beacon Press, 1988.

Sulloway, F.J. *Freud: biologist of the mind.* New York: Basic Books, 1983.

Suppe, F. *The structure of scientific theories.* 2nd edition. Urbana: University of Illinois Press, 1977.

Taussig, M.T. *The devil and commodity fetishism in South America.* Chapel Hill: University of North Carolina Press, 1980.

Taylor-Gooby, P. "Personal consumption and gender." 274–284. *Sociology,* 19, no.2, 1985.

Thaler, R. "Toward a positive theory of consumer choice," *Journal of Economic Behavior and Organization,* (1980), Vol.1, 39–60.

Thompson, C. *Psychoanalysis: evolution and development.* New York: Hermitage House, 1951.

Tice, D.M., E. Bratislavsky, and R.F. Baumeister. "Emotional distress regulation takes precedence over impulse control: if you feel bad, do it!" *Journal of Personality and Social Psychology,* (2001), 80, part 1, 53–67.

Timpano, K.R., et al. "The epidemiology of the proposed DSM-5 hoarding disorder: exploration of the acquisition specifier, associated features, and distress," *Journal of Clinical Psychiatry,* (2011), 76, no.6, 780–786.

———, et al. "General life stress and hoarding: examining the role of emotional tolerance," *International Journal of Cognitive Therapy,* (2011), 4, no.3, 263–279.

Tolin, D.F., G. Steketee, R. Frost. *Buried in treasures: help for compulsive acquiring, saving, and hoarding.* New York: Oxford University Press, 2006.

——— "The economic and social burden of compulsive hoarding," *Psychiatry Research,* (2008), 60, no.2, 200–211.

Tolin, D.F., et al. "An exploratory study of the neural mechanisms of decision making in compulsive hoarding," *Psychological Medicine,* (2009), 39, no.2, 325–336.

——— . "Understanding and treating hoarding: a biopsychosocial perspective," *Journal of Clinical Psychology,* (2011), 67, no.5, 517–526.

—— et al., "Neural mechanisms of decision making in hoarding disorder," *Archive of General Psychiatry,* (2012), 69, no.8, 832–841.

Tomkins, M.A., T. Hartl, and R. Frost. *Digging out: helping your loved one manage clutter, hoarding, and compulsive acquiring.* Oakland: New Harbinger Publications, 2009.

Tversky, A and D. Kahneman. "The framing of decisions and the psychology of choice," *Science,* (1981), 211, no4481, 453–458.

Toulmin, G. "The logical status of psychoanalysis." 23–29. *Analysis,* 9, 1948.

Twenge, J.M. and W.K. Campbell, *The narcissism epidemic: living in the age of entitlement.* New York: Free Press, 2009.

Valverde, M. *Diseases of the will: alcohol and dilemmas of freedom.* Cambridge: Cambridge University Press, 1998.

Vohs, K. and R.J. Faber. "Spent resources: self-regulatory resource availability affects impulse buying," *Journal of Consumer Research,* (2007), 33, no.1, 537–547.

Vohs, K. and Baumeister, R. *Handbook of self-regulation: research, theory and application.* (eds.), 2nd edition, New York: Guilford Press, 2013.

Vries, J. de. *The industrious revolution: consumer behavior and the household economy.* Cambridge: Cambridge University Press, 2008.

Wagner, C.C., and K.S. Ingersoll. *Motivational interviewing in groups.* New York: Guilford Pres, 2013.

Watson, G. "Disordered appetites: addiction, compulsion and dependence," In. J. Elster (ed.). *Addictions: entries and exists.* (1999), New York: Sage, 3–28.

Wesson, C. *Women who shop too much: overcoming the urge to splurge.* New York: St. Martin's Press, 1990.

Wilder, A. *System and structure.* 2nd. edition. London: Tavistock, 1984.

Wilson, T. and D. Gilbert. "Affective forecasting: knowing what to want," *Current Directions in Psychological Science,* (2005), 14, no.3, 131–134.

Winestine, M.C. "Compulsive shopping as a derivative of a childhood seduction." (1985) *Psychoanalytic Quarterly,* 54, no.1, 70–72.

Winsberg, M.E., K.S. Cassic, & M. Koran. "Hoarding in obsessive-compulsive disorder: a report of 20 cases," *Journal of Clinical Psychiatry,* (1999), 60, no9, 591–597.

Winslow, E.G. "Keynes and Freud: psychoanalysis and Keynes's account of the 'animal spirits' of capitalism," *Social Research,* (1986), 53, no.4, 549–578.

Winston, G.C. "Addiction and backsliding: a theory of compulsive consumption." 295–324. *Journal of Economic Behavior and Organization.* 1, 1980.

Wittgenstein, L. *Lectures and conversations.* Edited by C. Barrett. Berkeley: University of California Press, 1967.

——*Culture and value.* Edited by G.H. von Wright. Chicago: University f Chicago Press, 1984.

Wolff, R.P. *Moneybags must be so lucky.* Amherst: University of
Massachusetts Press, 1988.

Wollheim, R. (ed.). *Freud: a collection of critical essays.* New York:
Anchor Books, 1974.

Woolfolk, R.L. *The cure of souls: science, values, and psychotherapy.*
San Francisco: Jossy-Bass Publishers, 1998.

Workman, L. and D. Paper. "Compulsive buying: a theoretical
framework," *The Journal of Business Inquiry,* (2010), 9, no.1,
89–126.

Yankelovitch, D. & W. Barrett, *Ego and instinct.* New York: Vintage
Books, 1971.

Acknowledgements

This book could not have been written without the assistance of many individuals. I wish to thank my research advisor at the Smith College School for Social Work, Dr. Edmund DeLacour. Among the countless workshop leaders I've had the pleasure to study with, I want to single out Dr. Aaron Beck and the Beck Institute for Cognitive-Behavioral Therapy, Gail Steketee, Randy Frost, Marni Mcdonald, Christiana Bratiotis, Jessie Edsell Vetter, Philip Cushman, Simon Critchley, David Tolin, and Gary Patronek.

Among the many philosophers that I have had the honor to study with, Alasdair MacIntyre was a profound influence on this book. Professor Gerald Izenberg has been a true mentor as a historian of ideas, especially on Freud and Freudian existentialists. I hold a strong debt of gratitude to Dianne Sandman, Senior Paralegal, Community Legal Aid for her leadership role in providing services and education on the many problems associated with hoarding disorder. All psychotherapists are deeply indebted to the legion of suffering souls who have educated us about the many layers of suffering caused by compulsive disorders.

Finally, I dedicate this book to my wonderful wife, Marjorie, without whose encouragement, technical and creative support, this book would never have been finished.

Index

www.ingramcontent.com/pod-product-compliance
Lightning Source LLC
Chambersburg PA
CBHW071330280526
45787CB00001B/51